How to Write a
GREAT
BUSINESS PLAN
for Your Small Business in
60 MINUTES
OR LESS

Sharon L. Fullen
Dianna Podmoroff, BA, MBA, CHRP

How to Write a Great Business Plan
for Your Small Business in 60 Minutes or Less

1210 SW 23rd Place • Ocala, Florida 34474 • 800-814-1132 • 352-622-5836–Fax
Web site: www.atlantic-pub.com • E-mail sales@atlantic-pub.com
SAN Number :268-1250

ISBN-13: 978-0-910627-56-6
ISBN-10: 0-910627-56-8
Library of Congress Cataloging-in-Publication Data

Fullen, Sharon L.
  How to write a great business plan for your small business in 60 minutes or less / Sharon Fullen.
    p. cm.
  Includes index.
  ISBN 0-910627-56-8 (alk. paper)
  1. Small business--Planning. 2. New business enterprises. I. Title.

  HD62.7.F855 2005
  658.1'141--dc22
                        2005015286
Printed in the United States

ART DIRECTION & INTERIOR DESIGN: Meg Buchner • megadesn@mchsi.com
FRONT COVER DESIGN: Jackie Miller
BOOK PRODUCTION DESIGN: Laura Siitari of Siitari by Design • www.siitaribydesign.com

TABLE OF CONTENTS

CHAPTER 7　MANAGEMENT SUMMARY

CHAPTER 8　FINANCIAL PLAN

CHAPTER 9　PUT IT ALL TOGETHER

CHAPTER 10　RESEARCHING YOUR PLAN

CHAPTER 11　WRITING TIPS

GLOSSARY

INDEX

INTRODUCTION

S *tarting your own business* is an exciting
adventure. Close your eyes and visualize how
the showroom looks, dream of the latest high-tech
equipment, imagine the sounds of a busy store, taste
your signature dish, and see the faces of satisfied
customers. Now think about writing a business
plan for your new business. The reverie is over,
right? Take a deep breath; help is on the way. *How
to Write a Great Business Plan for Your Small Business
in 60 Minutes or Less* was written to give first-time
entrepreneurs as well as seasoned business owners
the support and guidance they need to write a
practical, no-nonsense business plan in 60 minutes
or less! This is your **FAST PLAN**.

While some consider writing a business plan a necessary evil in order to secure financing from a banker or investor, you need to realize that your business plan is far more than a fancy sales tool; it is a powerful management tool to help you set objectives, focus on your goals, and avoid potential pitfalls. The process of writing a business plan enables you to consider all the aspects of starting a business — ranging from identifying opportunities to exploring risks to putting dollar amounts to ideas; the business plan makes you think about the highs and the lows, the advantages and the disadvantages, and the potential for success and failure. Although there are businesses that are successful without a business plan, significantly more businesses that fail to plan also fail to succeed.

The concepts and tools presented in the **FAST PLAN** approach can be used to expand any or all of the facets of a business plan to create a dynamic and powerful tool for complete business evaluation. If you are uncertain whether your **FAST PLAN** meets your needs, have a trusted banker, businessperson, or advisor review it before you depend on it to obtain financing. To find local advisors, check the last chapter for national organizations that provide support for entrepreneurs.

To help you create your **FAST PLAN**, an excerpt from a real business plan is included at the end of each business plan section. Use the information in the chapters and the real-life application to help tailor your **FAST PLAN**. For more guidance and examples, there is also a complete business plan titled "Down by the River" included in Chapter 13.

LOOK FOR THE FAST PLAN ICON

If the *60 Minutes or Less* part of the title is what made you buy this book, you probably don't want to spend days learning how to write a business plan or devote lots of late-night hours to the process.

This is why each chapter has **FAST PLAN** tips—just look for the following icon:

If you know what you are looking for, then go to the **Fast Plan** Table of Contents, find the **FAST PLAN** clock icon, and skip right to the section. This book covers all you need to know to research and write a business plan.

TABLE OF CONTENTS

CHAPTER 1   PREPARING TO PLAN

CHAPTER 2   WRITING YOUR BUSINESS PLAN

CHAPTER 3   BUSINESS OVERVIEW/COMPANY SUMMARY

PREPARING TO PLAN

Writing a complex, formal business plan** can take several days, weeks, or even months. From research through printing the last page, the time you take depends upon the research you need, your writing skills, and available time and supporting analysis required. It isn't uncommon for an inexperienced entrepreneur to become bogged down and lost in the whole process.

With a **FAST PLAN**, the process is streamlined, concentrating on the most critical aspects of a successful business plan. To complete your **FAST PLAN**, you will likely need to do some research beyond what you know already, and the amount of time required will depend on your current business skill level, industry experience, and ability to create projections. Each chapter in this book provides in-depth guidance so you'll always have answers at hand.

YOUR BUSINESS CONCEPT

Before you can start your **FAST PLAN**, you need to decide what you want to accomplish with your business. What is your business idea about? The best way to do this is to start writing. Thinking about your concept is important, but taking the time to write your concept makes it real, and that reality can then be critically analyzed.

Use the following outline to write your concept. This concept will be used and expanded on throughout your **FAST PLAN**, so be as specific as possible in simple-to-understand terms.

DEVELOP YOUR BUSINESS CONCEPT

Business Name

> (general concept/idea)

Specifically, we will provide:

Business Concept

> (describe the business opportunity and why you
>   want to start this particular business)

Services

> (describe your services)

Products

> (describe your products)

We will provide these products and/or services to:

> (describe your customers)

Once you have your business concept well defined, you need to condense the concept into its most salient points. Often you will have only a minute or two to sell someone on your idea, so you need to convey your idea succinctly, clearly highlighting its most compelling aspects. To do this, you need to create an "elevator pitch."

ELEVATOR PITCH

The elevator pitch is a brief description that takes no longer than an elevator ride to deliver. It neatly sums up what you want to offer (your business concept), capturing the excitement and potential of your idea.

Example Opening:

"I'm opening a restaurant featuring exquisite dinners from every region of China. I've hired a chef from a popular New York establishment, and renowned restaurant designer Barbara Lazaroff is working on the interior design."

To help you write your elevator pitch, imagine you are alone in an elevator with billionaire Donald Trump. Here is your chance to pitch your idea to him. Can you capture his attention, sell him on your idea, and engage his entrepreneurial spirit before you reach the twenty-second floor?

Focus on facts that answer the following questions:

Questions	Examples
How will you deliver the goods and services?	Sell products with free installation, mobile repair shop.
How will you attract your potential customers?	Direct mail campaigns, freeway sign.
Where will you be located?	A mall kiosk, Web site.
How will you find customers?	Office complex workers, local high school.
With whom will you be in business?	Four partners, sole proprietorship.
Whom will you hire with special experience, talents, or connections?	Renowned architect, skilled chef.
When will you launch?	Date (rationale).
When will you need investment monies?	Stage two of product development.
Do you believe you are better than the competition?	Unique features, specialties.
Why do you think you will be successful?	Unfulfilled need, trend, solution.

DEVELOP YOUR ELEVATOR PITCH

Elevator Pitch
Describe, in only 150 words and 60 seconds, everything most prospective investors would want to know before asking to see your business plan:

- Your company.

- Your product.

- Your market.

- Your market/product differentiation; that is, "Why us?"

- Your revenue model.

- Your personal qualifications.

- How much money you need.

- What you would do with the money if you get it?

Your elevator pitch is a useful tool that helps you focus on your goals. At the end of your elevator pitch, make sure you ask for something. You never know who might be able to solve a problem, refer you to someone else, or offer invaluable advice. Here are a few examples of what you might ask:

- "Do you know anyone in the gift industry who could represent my imported line?"

- "Have you found a 'Big Bank Officer'

interested in small business startup loans?"

- "I'm looking for investors in my new widget. Would you be interested in learning the details? Do you know anyone else who might be interested?"

In fact, your entire business plan focuses on what you need to be successful. Financial resources are important, but so are knowledge and people resources. Whether you need $50,000 seed money, sweat-equity partners, or good advice, ask for what you want.

Before we get too far into the process, there are some conventions for writing business plans that you need to know. Most people will not read your business plan; they will merely skim it. For that reason, your plan needs to be written clearly and concisely, with crisp and direct language.

Critical messages should not be buried in lengthy paragraphs. You may believe that pages and pages of business strategies and financial plans are what you need to convince people to invest, but more often, the opposite is true. Stick to a classic business plan format.

Ultimately, your plan has to address the needs of the reader and answer that quintessential question: "What's in it for me?". Address as many arguments as you can, and always present your information with the end-user in mind.

Because the goal of many business plans is to secure a loan or investment capital, it is tempting to paint an overly optimistic scenario. Don't do it. Savvy lenders and investors know what is typical in various industries, and they are experienced readers of financial reports. Inflated profits and unrealistic projections will not win you confidence, nor will they provide you with the information you need to make good business decisions and become successful.

Remember, you and your business concept are judged for suitability, profitability, and potential. If it appears that your expectations or projections are unrealistic, the conclusion may be that your business skills are insufficient, that you are a dishonest person, or that your concept is lacking.

RULES FOR WRITING A BUSINESS PLAN

1. Write clearly and concisely.

2. Follow a proven business plan format.

3. Address the answer to the reader's ultimate question: "What's in it for me?"

4. Present the facts honestly.

5. Present your expectations realistically.

WHAT DOES A BUSINESS PLAN DO?

As you begin exploring the possibilities of opening a new business or enhancing your current business, ideas, emotions, and dreams fill your head. Should you do this, or would that be better? With so many things to think about, where do you start? The answers to these questions and many more are found within the entrepreneur's best guide and decision-making tool—the business plan!

I don't know too many people who are excited about the prospect of writing their business plans. It requires doing extensive research, asking many questions, calculating projected financial statements, and doing some real soul searching. Nevertheless, the benefits are worth the effort. Once you get everything down on paper, you'll be better prepared to handle a multitude of business situations.

PURPOSES OF YOUR BUSINESS PLAN

1. Describe your new or existing business.

2. Define your customers' needs and your ability to meet those needs.

3. Explore competitors' strengths and weaknesses.

4. Address possible obstacles to success.

5. Establish yourself and your team as capable businesspeople.

6. Detail marketing strategies to capture a share of the market.

7. Set benchmarks and goals for launching, developing, and profit making.

8. Provide financial projections and returns on investment.

9. Ask for money to support your success.

10. Inform investors and lenders of "what's in it for them."

In the following chapters, you'll learn how to develop a **FAST PLAN** that addresses all ten of these purposes.

Remember, your plan is a collection of information and ideas based upon your knowledge, expertise, background, and faith at the time. As you move through each stage of your business development, you'll learn new facts and gain additional experience that may alter your path and goals.

WHY DO YOU NEED A PLAN?

You need a business plan to explore your business ideas and to determine their viability as well as to secure money to make your ideas happen. Most people concentrate on the last reason — to get money. Their plan, then, is written solely to attract outside investors or satisfy lender requirements. If you write your plan primarily for them, you may risk "slanting the truth" while you overlook other areas that could benefit you.

Researching and writing a business plan offers multiple benefits for new and experienced business owners. The process of developing the plan helps solidify your desires and set your professional goals. Writing your plan will:

Clarify Your Vision

Instead of just saying, "I'd like to own a business," you'll be creating a Technicolor® version of your business, whether it's a cozy Italian deli, a prosperous lawn maintenance service, or an in-demand massage therapy service.

Prove Your Potential

You'll prove to yourself and others that your community needs another pool-service company or a state-of-the-art gym. On the other hand, you may discover that your idea isn't a viable one. Too much competition, the wrong location, an inadequate customer base, or insufficient customer demand are all reasons to reassess your ideas.

Look at Obstacles

Every business venture will have obstacles. By looking at potential problems and outlining solutions before they happen, you can lessen the impact those events will have on your business. Not all problem/solution scenarios will make it into your plan, but you'll uncover many of them as you research your business prospects.

Determine Your Business Viability

Are your goals achievable with the people, time, and money resources you have available to you? Is the idea too trendy? Will it have sufficient lifespan to repay lenders? Will investors be attracted to the idea?

Project Your Success

Will your business idea provide you with the personal and financial rewards you are seeking? Can you physically or emotionally deal with the workload? Do you have sufficient experience to make it happen?

Secure Ample Capital

By projecting your cash flow and working capital needs, you'll have a better understanding of how much money you will have to pay your vendors, lenders, and employees. Before you invest your entire nest egg or borrow money, you must decide if you'll have enough money (from every possible source) to keep you afloat until your business begins to make a profit. Insufficient capital is a primary reason new businesses fail.

Sometimes the act of writing your business plan and crunching the numbers proves that your idea is not profitable or that it will not provide sufficient profit for long-term sustainability. It's much better to discover that before you invest the time and energy starting a business than to discover it six months or a year into the venture, after you've accumulated new debt and have no means to repay it. Your business plan then becomes a vehicle for you to regroup and adjust your strategy to address the shortfalls identified in the original plan. You may decide to continue or you may start fresh with a new idea. Either way, the process of writing your business plan could very well save you from potential financial ruin, long-term debt, and the accompanying stress.

WHO WILL READ YOUR BUSINESS PLAN?

Potential investors (family members, friends, and outside professionals) will need a copy of your plan to review the profitability potential of your business. Lenders (banks, credit unions, government agencies, family members, and friends) will also need a copy to determine your ability to repay loans. Both investors and lenders will look at your idea along with your financial projections.

Your insurance agent may want to see sections of your plan to determine your needs for liability, auto, fire, casualty, theft, and life insurance.

Your real estate broker may want to see sections of your plan to help you locate the right property (land or land and building) for your new business. Your architect and builder/contractor may also want to review parts of your plan before designing a new building, planning renovations, or specifying remodeling projects. Other designers (landscape, interior, kitchen, lighting, sound) will also benefit from looking over your business plan.

Confidentiality/Non-Disclosure Agreements

The information you gather and report in your business plan is confidential. Although it may not be "top secret," it is in your best interest to have certain parties sign a non-disclosure agreement before receiving your plan to read. A non-disclosure agreement outlines that the information is proprietary and confidential and is not to be shared, copied, distributed, or discussed with unauthorized parties. This agreement can be verbal or written. Should a violation of the agreement occur, a written agreement offers you the best protection.

Please note: Bankers, lenders, and venture capitalists are professionals bound to confidentiality. Requiring a non-disclosure agreement (and/or contract clause) from them is generally considered insulting and unprofessional.

WHAT INTERESTED PARTIES SHOULD FIND IN YOUR PLAN

Everyone who reads your business plan will be looking for something different based upon his or her needs. The messages within your plan are largely what sell your concept. This is the soul of your business, and it affects how people respond to your requests for support. Even bankers, who want to see strong financials, are looking for a "gut reaction" that tells them you and your idea are worth the investment.

Your Family

Your first support group should be your family members. Even if yours isn't intended to be a family business, it will, at least initially, put additional demands on everyone, requiring you to work long hours, distracting you from family activities, and generally creating stress. Include your extended family in your vision and let them read your plan. Your family should see both why your dream is important to you and how they can take an active role in its success.

Your Partners

Whether you have a silent or active partnership arrangement, everyone should share the vision expressed in the plan. If you have an active partner, write the plan together. Contributions from everyone are respected and valued, and that should come across in the business plan. Your partner's role in the business should provide more than money — it should fulfill entrepreneurial dreams as well.

Your Lenders

Family members and friends. Borrowing from family members and friends can be an excellent way to finance your business launch or growth. Although you may not have a lengthy loan application, you should treat these loans just as seriously as you would a bank loan. Private lenders should be able to see that they are making a loan that can be repaid.

Bankers. Your banker can be much more than a source of credit. Many banks offer individualized business banking services that will save you time and money, so building a relationship is important. Bankers should see that your business has ample capital and resources for continuous operation over several months (possibly more than a year) and sufficient profits to pay back your loan on time.

Private organizations. Depending upon your

community economic level, you may qualify for financial support in the way of low-interest loans or grants (essentially a financial gift) through privately funded organizations and associations. These funds are typically used to stimulate economic development in high-risk communities or economic parity for women and minorities. Check your local business development agency to see if they have a list of private loans and grant programs. Philanthropic organizations should see that you, your community, and your company meet their criteria for economic support. They will consider your ability to repay your loan. If you are applying for a grant, they will examine your potential for success, contribution to the community (creating jobs, paying taxes, and rejuvenating neighborhoods), and need.

Government agencies. Several national, state, and county agencies can provide you with loans and grants, providing your business meets their criteria. The Small Business Administration (SBA) run by the federal government is a major supporter of small businesses. Government agencies should see that your business would be capable of repaying loans. Grant applications will be reviewed for their ability to satisfy the grant program's mission.

Your Investors

Any person or business that gives you money in

exchange for a share of ownership is an investor. An investor can be a family member or a friend, an angel investor, or a venture capitalist. Ownership requires a greater risk, so this money will "cost" you more than financing. Investors should see that your business has an excellent profit potential. A plan that doesn't demonstrate an ample return on their investment may not be worth their time. They'll also want to see that you and your team have the ability to start and operate a successful business.

Your Employees

Employees' energy, enthusiasm, expertise, and ideas are the foundation of your business. If you have an existing business, involve your staff in the development or update of your business plan. Not only can you tap into their skills and expertise, but you also empower them to think creatively and to "own" the idea. This ownership mentality is invaluable in achieving your goals and creating a successful business. Your employees should see how they can make a difference, what your mutual goals are, and how you can actively support one another. Your plan can also establish success benchmarks, business guidelines, and employee performance standards.

Your Suppliers

As a new business, establishing yourself with vendors can be an arduous task. Even existing businesses often have failed to develop strong partnerships with their suppliers. You may find it advantageous to share sections of your business plan with select vendors. Solid companies want to build long-term relationships with trusted customers, and sharing your vision and potential may be a way to start that relationship. Your suppliers should see the fiscal wisdom of your endeavor and see the payoff (in long-term business with increasing purchase volume).

HOW YOUR BUSINESS PLAN WILL BE ASSESSED

To save yourself time, you must consider the way lenders and investors will assess your plan. You need to concentrate on what they need. Before you start researching and writing, read this list to make certain your plan addresses each concept below.

12 QUESTIONS YOUR PLAN MUST ANSWER

Does your plan:

1. **Tell the story of your vision in a clear, concise manner that is backed by facts?**

   - Include your dreams, but don't rely on superlatives and opinions that cannot be supported.

   - Remember, every business says it is the best, its quality is excellent, and its service is unequalled. You need to include ways to demonstrate those assertions.

2. **Describe a marketable idea based upon your dreams and supported with facts?**

   • Provide proof that customers want your products or services and are willing to buy them at a profitable price.

3. **Promote a few solid products/services?**

   • Focus on starting small and growing. Doing too much too fast can drain you financially, physically, and emotionally, setting the stage for failure.

   • Become an expert on your products and services, allowing yourself time to develop a healthy business before expanding.

4. **Explain long-term benefits?**

   • Promote such benefits as environmentally friendly packaging or energy-efficient manufacturing processes.

   • Explain how you will eliminate potential risks or harmful aspects through such attributes as childproof, biodegradable, or recyclable packaging.

5. **Describe workable strategies and goals for launching and developing your business?**

   - Define your ideas: create practical strategies, achievable goals, realistic deadlines, and measurements of success.

   - Look at ways to deal with unexpected issues and discuss your preparedness in a positive way.

6. **Detail a clearly defined target market of ample size and buying power to be profitable?**

   - Know who your customers are and why they are your ideal customers.

   - Don't rely on "selling everything to everyone."

   - Develop a large enough target market for continued growth.

7. **Talk about your competitive advantage?**

   - Look for ways to outperform your competition and develop your own unique brand identity.

   - Can you exploit a rival's weakness?

- Are you merely "riding on someone else's reputation" or hoping to siphon off customers without doing anything different?

8. **Include managers, key personnel, and support staff with the skills and experience to make your business a success?**

   - Many small businesses rely on family and friends, which can be a benefit if they are qualified.

   - Remember, investors and lenders invest in people, not only ideas.

9. **Outline your ability to control the quality and ability to deliver your products?**

   - One of the worst situations a new business can find itself in is to have more orders than they can supply.

   - If you depend on outside vendors or manufacturers for raw materials or wholesale products, will you be able to maintain consistent quality and recover should they fail as suppliers?

10. **Show realistic financial projections and include best-case, most likely, and worst-case scenarios?**

- Base your business on solid expectations, not on "what ifs" and circumstances you cannot control.

- Best-case scenarios can be achievable, but the most likely scenario is where you should focus.

- Worst-case scenarios won't scare investors and lenders away if you approach them reasonably and have built-in ways to overcome unexpected setbacks.

11. **Demonstrate profitability in a relatively short period?**

   - The quicker you can break even and begin making a profit, the lower your risk factor.

   - Will your business be able to provide a large enough return to attract investors?

12. **Show that you have made a personal investment?**

   - A plan backed only by ideas and sweat equity (unpaid time you personally devote) is considered to be a high risk.

   - If you do not have 100 percent of the financing required to launch your business, that's okay. Investors and lenders are looking for an appropriate financial stake that you will share with them.

After you've finished your **FAST PLAN**, make sure that potential investors and lenders have everything they need to know to make a favorable decision.

chapter 2

WRITING YOUR BUSINESS PLAN

A *good business plan contains* dreams and ideas backed by facts and figures presented in a standardized format. The standard format makes it easier for lenders and investors (who look at hundreds and even thousands of business plans every month) to scan for specific information efficiently. Lenders may just skim your plan and assign it to a lower-level employee who will read it thoroughly.

Investors, with more demanding criteria for funding, may not actually read your plan at all. They will be checking specific sections for the potential return on their investment. Your financial reports and projections will provide them with enough information to reject your request, refer the plan to a subordinate for a full follow-up, or read it in full.

STANDARD BUSINESS PLAN FORMAT

There are specific sections that must be included in your business plan; however, the order and presentation may be varied to best explain your business and its unique situation. You may find sample plans with different section titles, but essentially all the information will be there; your job is to choose a format that best highlights your business opportunity. A comprehensive plan will include the following categories:

I.   Executive Summary

II.   Business Overview/Company Summary

III.   Products and Services

IV.   Industry Overview/Market Analysis

V.   Marketing Strategy and Implementation

VI.   Management Summary

VII.   Financial Plan

VIII. Summary

IX.   Supporting Documents

The companion CD included with this book contains templates and examples of the main sections included in a business plan. For more information on the CD and other business plan software, see Chapter 12 – *Business Plan Software*.

As you think about your business idea and prepare to write your plan, try to maintain an objective point of view. Think about your business from the viewpoint of a stranger. What would you want to know if you were going invest in a business? Think about the facts you would need to convince someone to write that check.

FAST PLAN PREPARATION

Quick and Dirty Business Plan Q&A

In order to write a **FAST PLAN**, you must have a clear sense of your business opportunity. Before you sit down to write your plan, prepare and condense your thoughts and ideas by answering the following questions. Use no more than one or two paragraphs, and use facts to support your claims.

1. What are you selling? Product? Service? Both?

2. Why this product or service?

3. What is your market?

4. Who will need and buy your product or

service?

5. Will there be enough buyers to turn a profit? Future profits?

6. Can you be profitable?

7. Are profits ample enough to offset risks?

8. Can you control and maintain quality, service and delivery?

9. Who are you and your team? Are you capable of making this business successful?

10. What's in it for the reader (investor or lender)?

11. Why should the reader read this business plan?

In the following chapters, you will walk through the creation of a **FAST PLAN** business plan. When the plan is broken down into manageable pieces, it is not an intimidating task. You can quickly articulate your thoughts with a small amount of planning and preparation. Included are lists of common mistakes to avoid.

To help you understand and apply the concepts presented, follow the fictitious company Advanced Business Solutions as it creates its own **FAST PLAN** business plan. An excerpt from Advanced Business

Solution's business plan will follow each section of the **FAST PLAN**. Using the information in the chapters, the templates on the companion CD, the sample business plan excerpts, and the complete business plan found at the end of this book, you will be able to write a comprehensive, intelligent, and compelling business plan that will help bring your vision to life.

MISTAKES TO AVOID

- **Waiting until the last minute.** Even though you want to write a **FAST PLAN**, give yourself time to think, prepare, and gather the information you'll need. Waiting until the last minute puts you under pressure and makes it harder to write.

- **Forgetting to tailor your FAST PLAN for a specific purpose.** Creating a generic, all-purpose plan may be easier, but will it answer the reader's ultimate question, "What's in it for me?"

- **Assuming prior knowledge.** Don't assume the reader understands what you are selling. Be specific and concise in your descriptions.

- **Saying things you don't believe.** Insincerity is easy to recognize.

chapter 3

BUSINESS OVERVIEW/
COMPANY SUMMARY

The purpose of the **Business Overview**, or Company Summary, is to provide readers with an overall feel for what you are trying to accomplish with this venture. In addition, it outlines what you have done so far in the process. This section comes after the Executive Summary (which we will write last) and is geared toward giving the reader a detailed look at your vision by providing information about your mission and objectives as well as who will own the company and where it will be located.

BUSINESS HISTORY

This section should describe the overall picture, from the time the business was started (if started prior to writing your business plan) to where your business is presently. Outline the work you have done so far as well as any sales you have made to date.

Excerpt Alert

Business History

Advanced Business Solutions is a management consulting business that began operations on February 3, 2006. Advanced Business Solutions is a sole proprietorship, owned by J. Jaxson. J. Jaxson has extensive experience and training in management and business solutions. This home-based consulting service will target local businesses in need of expert, professional, affordable management consultation or support on a short-term or contractual basis.

MISSION STATEMENT

Your mission statement, or statement of purpose, is similar to the objective section of a résumé. This statement should capture the reasons why you want to be in business, what you want to accomplish with your business, who your business serves, and how your company will benefit others.

Write Your Mission Statement

1. Start with your elevator pitch. Keep it as short as possible; no more than three or four sentences.

2. Write clearly and concisely.

3. Be straightforward and realistic.

4. Avoid such superlatives as "unequalled service" or "greatest product ever sold."

5. Think about what you want your customers to receive from visiting your business, receiving your service, or purchasing your products. Some examples:

   a. You want them to be physically and emotionally satisfied.

   b. You want them to experience the pleasure of pampering.

   c. You want them to have fun.

   d. You want them to feel safe.

6. Look at sample mission statements for creative stimulus. However, don't take one as your own, as it simply won't capture the essence of your plan's message.

7. Read *Creating Mission Statements for Smaller Groups* by Beverly Goldberg ($3.95 PDF download at **Amazon.com**).

Excerpt Alert

Mission Statement

To provide professional management consulting and business services that enable clients to identify and capitalize on opportunities and achieve their operational goals.

BUSINESS GOALS AND OBJECTIVES

Your business goals and objectives will cover your short-term (within one year) and long-term (within two to five years) expectations as a business owner and an entrepreneur. Think of goals as your dreams with a deadline, and your objectives as the way you will achieve those goals. Your goals are typically measured in revenue, store traffic, or other tangible results.

Common types of business goals:

1. Increased sales volume.

2. Decreased number of hours the owner(s) works.

3. Greater number of customers.

4. Increased market share.

5. Higher profit levels.

6. Increased workforce.

7. Greater cash flow.

8. Expansion (additional stores or larger business facility).

Write Your Objectives

Objectives are the steps you will take to achieve these goals. These are also measurable activities that answer the who, what, how, why, and when questions. For example:

Who = Management team

What = Increase customer returns

How = Customer service weekly training

Why = Satisfied customers create repeat customers

When = Three-month review and assessment

For example: Your first goal—the launch of your new business—is detailed below.

Short-Term

Goal #1—Official business opening date of November 5.

Goal #2—Hire general manager to assist with overseeing complete renovation of leased building.

Goal #3—Hire general contractor with business remodeling experience.

Goal #4—Obtain $50,000 capital equipment loan.

Long-Term

Goal # 5—Open second business in local suburb in year three.

Goal #6—Cash reserves of $150,000 to be set aside for expansion funding.

Goal #7—Set monthly savings goals to raise additional $150,000 in eight months.

Goal #8—Create training/mentoring program for assistant manager to be responsible for outfitting and starting second location.

Start by creating three to five short-term goals and outline how you will achieve these. Be realistic and use your financial projections to benchmark and support your ability to reach each goal. Your objectives should be realistic for a business owner. Set business and personal goals that are attainable despite the daily requirements of being in business for yourself.

Excerpt Alert

Objectives

The primary objectives over the next year are to:

- Start up and begin operation of Advanced Business Solutions.

- Generate one to three new contracts per month by distributing a detailed business package to key local businesses and associations, networking with key business leaders, joining relevant business associations, and advertising in local newspapers.

- Join a Web-based contract procurement service and obtain one new Internet-serviced client per month.

- Generate a net profit of $XXXXXX [use a real number here] in the first year of operations with a positive cash flow by developing a strong client base and keeping overhead costs to a minimum.

BUSINESS OWNERSHIP

In this section, you will describe your legal form of business and ownership. Ownership percentages and participation requirements will be included here as well. Your accountant and/or attorney can advise the best form for your business both to protect yourself from personal financial risks and to obtain the greatest tax benefits. For more information on business structures and do-it-yourself incorporation, see Chapter 12 – *Business Plan References.*

Sole Proprietorship — The easiest and least expensive way of starting a business.

> A sole proprietorship can be formed by simply finding a location and opening the door for business. Start-up attorney's fees will be less than those of other business types. The owner has absolute authority over all business decisions. The biggest negative to sole proprietorship is personal liability should the business default on a loan or be involved in a legal dispute.

Partnership — Two or more parties that join to share ownership.

> The two most common partnership types are general and limited. A general partnership can be formed simply by an oral agreement between two or more persons, but a legal partnership agreement drawn up by an attorney is highly recommended. Legal fees for drawing up a partnership agreement are higher than those for a sole proprietorship, but may be lower than incorporating. A partnership agreement could be helpful in solving any disputes. However, partners are responsible for the other partners' business actions, as well as their own.

Corporation — Business entity where control depends upon stock ownership.

A business may incorporate without an attorney, but legal advice is highly recommended. The corporate structure is usually the most complex and is more costly to organize. Control depends on stock ownership. Persons with the largest stock ownership, not the total number of shareholders, control the corporation. Small, closely held corporations can operate more informally, but recordkeeping cannot be eliminated. Officers of a corporation can be liable to stockholders for improper actions. Liability is generally limited to stock ownership, except where fraud is involved. You may want to incorporate as a "C" or "S" corporation, which require consultation with a professional.

Limited Liability Company (LLC) — Blends the benefits of a corporation with a sole proprietorship or partnership.

An LLC is not a corporation, but it offers many of the same advantages. Many small business owners and entrepreneurs prefer an LLC because they combine the limited liability protection of a corporation with the "pass through" taxation of a sole proprietorship or partnership. The main advantage an LLC has over incorporation is that it allows greater flexibility in management and business organization.

Excerpt Alert

Ownership

Advanced Business Solutions is a sole proprietorship, owned by J. Jaxson. As the business expands, strategic alliances may be formed with other consulting companies or business service providers.

LOCATION AND FACILITIES

The final portion of the Business Summary section is a description of where you plan to operate your business. Do you require retail space, a manufacturing facility, or an office?

In this section of your business plan, you'll describe why your chosen location and the facilities work for you and your customers. If your plan is seeking money for an expansion, you'll be detailing why the location could support the cost of an expansion and the return expected from increasing your facility's capacity. If you are buying unimproved land and are seeking construction financing, provide complete information on the land, zoning, and building design. Your feasibility studies may reveal that owning your own physical space requires too much start-up capital or would create too great of an initial debt burden.

Your customers may want to find you in a mall, in an office building, or sharing space with other complementary businesses. Typically, this means you'll be leasing space. Your contractual obligations along with your lease rate, rate increase provisions, or lessor-provided benefits will be discussed here. A long-term lease can be an advantage (stable expense and ability to build a local customer base) and a disadvantage (inability to relocate to accommodate a booming or declining business). Emphasize how leasing benefits your immediate financial situation and how you will deal with increased rates, exit clauses, or renewal potential.

Excerpt Alert

Location and Facilities

To keep overhead costs low, Advanced Business Solutions will be located in the home of J. Jaxson. The home, located at 1849 Upper McKinnon Road, is equipped with a computer, fax machine, and photocopier. J. Jaxson will supply her own administrative services. Where possible, all meetings and presentations will be held at the client's location. If this is not feasible, the company will rent a meeting room at the Morrison Community Centre as required. Presentation equipment, such as overhead projectors and liquid crystal display (LCD) units, will be rented from the Okanagan University College.

Any subcontractors hired for specific projects will not work in the office but from their own offices. This will greatly reduce overhead costs, allowing us to price our services competitively.

As Advanced Business Solutions grows, consideration will be given to acquiring office space.

MISTAKES TO AVOID

- **Relying on spell-checkers.** Where or wear, whose or who's, there or their, and other spelling and grammatical errors are easily missed by computer spell-checkers.

- **Too much jargon.** Minimize the industry-speak and technical jargon. Write for a professional business audience.

- **Too formal.** Many people believe that being professional means writing in a stilted formal style. Leave out words and phrases like "heretofore," "the party of the first part," and "aforementioned."

- **Touchy-feely writing**. The business plan for a mortuary and a flower shop won't have the same feel, and your plan should "sound" like your business; however, being too happy or overly optimistic can distract from the purpose of selling your idea.

chapter 4

PRODUCTS/SERVICES

In this section of the **FAST PLAN**, you will state clearly the important features of your products and/or services and their current stage of development, along with what will be needed to develop them fully and how the venture is expected to do that as well as or better than anyone else. Essentially, you are answering the question, "What makes your products and/or services unique or special?".

Most entrepreneurs rely on words to convey their product description, but a photograph or illustration of the product can be helpful. A prototype, particularly if the product is novel, will further enhance your presentation.

Discuss specific materials, manufacturing, and delivery methods. Tell the reader how these set you apart from competitors, why they are desired by customers, and how they increase your profit potential. Good marketing focuses on the benefits to the customers. Your plan should do likewise. No matter how excited about a specific product you are, unless it connects with buyers, it isn't a winner.

Your service style (self-serve, drive-thru, mobile, Web, brick-and-mortar store, etc.) is also a critical part of your product offering and a way to set your business apart from the competition. Discuss how these affect the product quality, your customer needs, and the overall profitability.

PRODUCT/SERVICE DESCRIPTION

A good place to begin defining what products you will sell and what services you will offer is to create a list of features and benefits. Features are what you offer customers, and benefits are what your customers receive from each feature. Benefits are the "what's in it for me" part of marketing your products and services.

When describing your products and services, you must address the features and emphasize the benefits side of the equation. I refer you to the following sales maxim that is often quoted:

"Unless the proposition appeals to their
 INTEREST, unless it satisfies their
 DESIRES, and unless it shows them a
 GAIN, then they will not buy!"

The easiest way to convert a feature into a benefit is to use the "which means…" transition. For instance, if you say your business is open 24 hours, that means you are offering convenience for people who need your product or service anytime. Here are a few examples of the features and benefits that a business might offer its customers.

Customer Features/Benefits

Feature	Benefit (Which means…)
Secure online ordering	Convenient 24/7 access with minimal privacy and security concerns.
Custom-decorated cakes	Easy to stop by and order a special-occasion cake. Create something personalized to suit the party.
Computerized buyer-loyalty program based on phone number	Easy savings and rewards loyalty. Convenient—no card to carry or special number to remember.
Delivery service	Save money—a trip to the store costs businesses "X" amount of dollars; helps them save time.

Excerpt Alert

Description of Products and Services

Advanced Business Solutions will devise successful corporate strategies and processes and assist organizations with meeting their operational goals. The primary types of customized services provided include Human Resource Management Consultation and Strategic Management Consultation.

Human Resource Management Consultation

Advanced Business Solutions will consult on a variety of human resource-related issues including:

- Recruitment and Selection
- Employee Development and Training
- Organizational Development and Effectiveness
- Employee or Labor Relations
- Compensation

Strategic Management Consultation

Advanced Business Solutions will help organizations:

- Identify and pursue strategic opportunities.
- Analyze current business systems (operational review).
- Develop new and more effective systems.
- Develop full business plans for start-up or existing businesses requiring financing, including introducing new products, entering new markets, and restructuring.

Key Features and Benefits of the Products and Services

Advanced Business Solutions will specialize in assisting businesses achieve their operational goals, whether that be by providing consultation to management, creating customized management solutions, or working on short-term specific tasks or projects necessary for the organization's success.

With today's unpredictable political and economic environments, it is increasingly difficult both for existing small- and medium-sized businesses to remain profitable and for entrepreneurs to successfully start new businesses. Advanced Business Solutions will address these needs by providing access to professional business expertise without the expense of hiring an employee or engaging a consultant. Advanced Business Solutions will offer creative, innovative, and effective solutions to business problems within the community.

Many consulting firms try to develop standard models to solve key business problems. Advanced Business Solutions has a variety of solutions: what may be right for one business would not necessarily meet the needs of another. Due to low overhead, Advanced Business Solutions will still be able to provide these customized solutions at reasonable rates.

PRODUCTION OF PRODUCTS AND SERVICES

This section will describe how your goods and/or services will be produced. Will everything be made in-house? What special equipment will be required? This section will be much more involved if you manufacture a product versus reselling products or selling services. Regardless, you must address the production issues fully. There are two types of production to consider: Sourcing and Fulfillment.

Product Sourcing

Finding a reliable source of product can be quite difficult. Four of the best ways to make contact with suppliers are trade shows, trade magazines, trade associations, and successful regional companies.

Trade shows

- Offer opportunities to spot upcoming trends.

- Provide networking opportunities with potential suppliers.

- Allow you to compare prices.

Trade magazines

- Offer an inexpensive way to find companies.

- Feature or mention companies that might offer the products you need.

- Provide information on upcoming trade shows and exhibits.

Trade associations

- Provide a valuable source of contacts.

- Include international companies.

- Match buyers with sellers.

Two resources for finding trade associations are:

1. Directory of Associations from Concept Marketing Group, Inc.: **www.marketingsource.com/associations**

2. *National Trade and Professional Associations of the United States 2004* edited by Buck Downs. Available on **www.amazon.com.**

Regional companies

Retail stores that are successful in one geographic area may not be able to expand because of resource constraints. Contact the owner to try to arrange a distributorship agreement.

Sourcing Considerations

1. Present yourself as a company and not a consumer.

2. Present yourself as someone who is seriously interested in building a business.

3. Increase your credibility by establishing yourself as a corporation.

4. Become a registered wholesaler to attract international firms.

5. Invest in samples.

6. Find at least two suppliers to ensure business continuity should one suffer a setback.

Product Fulfillment

Getting your product into the hands of customers raises several concerns. At first, you will likely handle much of the fulfillment process yourself, but as your company grows, it may become necessary to outsource this task. Fortunately, there are many companies that provide fulfillment services. What the reader of your business plan is looking for is whether you have taken the issue of order fulfillment into consideration, and whether you have adequately addressed immediate as well as short-, medium-, and long-term needs.

Excerpt Alert

Production of Products and Services

Initially all services will be performed by J. Jaxson. If a project's scope reaches beyond Ms. Jaxson's expertise or requires additional resources, subcontractors will be hired as needed to work on specific projects. Subcontractors will be hired based on their areas of expertise and experience and will be local whenever possible. Subcontractors will work from their own offices and will be linked directly to Advanced Business Solutions' office via e-mail and the Internet.

All reports will be produced and edited by J. Jaxson, and she will be responsible for the associated administrative tasks.

COMPETITIVE COMPARISON

In the Marketing section, your **FAST PLAN** will delve into great detail regarding competitors. However, a cursory discussion of a competitor's product/service offering is useful here to explain why you are entering the market and what you are proposing to do better than the competition.

To articulate how you differ from your competitors, use the following analysis as a guide:

Product or Service Analysis

Description

Describe what the product/service is and what it does.

_____

_____

_____

_____

_____

_____

Comparison

What advantages does your product/service have over those of the competition? What do you offer in unique features, expertise, or special training?

_____

_____

_____

_____

_____

_____

What disadvantages does it have?

_____

_____

_____

_____

_____

What special resources do you have to your
advantage? Consider name recognition, outstanding
product awards, and patent or franchiser's
trademark.

_____

_____

_____

_____

_____

_____

What obstacles or negative factors are associated
with your products? Are special permits or licenses
required? Will your product be affected by weather
or seasonality?

_____

_____

_____

_____

_____

_____

Excerpt Alert

Comparative Advantages in Production

The comparative advantages in production are low
overhead and labor costs. Advanced Business Solutions
does not have to pay for under-utilized staff or
facilities, and subcontractors will be hired as needed,
which means that the firm is not overstaffed during
downtimes.

FUTURE PRODUCTS AND SERVICES

In this section, you need to explore what your product/service mix will look like in the future. Will you be able to respond to trends? Will your customers want you to?

Excerpt Alert

Future Products and Services

Advanced Business Solutions will continually expand services based on industry trends and changing client needs. Advanced Business Solutions will not only solicit feedback from clients on what they may need in the future, but will also work to develop strong professional relationships with all clients.

Consideration will also be given to providing workshops or seminars on some of the identified key business issues facing organizations located in the Morrison, Pennsylvania, area.

Now that you have described your products and services, you are ready to introduce your readers to the Marketing Analysis portion of the **FAST PLAN**. No matter how great your product or service, unless you have surveyed the industry and analyzed the market opportunities, you have no idea if it will sell enough people at the right price for your business to be profitable.

You will have to spend time researching the industry, so look carefully at how to structure your research for optimum efficiency.

MISTAKES TO AVOID

- **Not clearly defining your products or services up front.** This should be a brief paragraph in your Executive Summary that an educated businessperson (outside of your industry) can understand. If the product or service is highly technical or requires a more detailed description, address that later in the plan.

- **Not identifying benefits.** Benefits are the reasons people buy. For example, a description is "waterproof," but the benefit is that construction workers don't have to remove it during inclement weather.

- **Not protecting intellectual property.** Failing to file for trademarks, service marks, patents, and copyrights is a costly mistake.

- **Relying on a single product.** Businesses that last start with a single great product but without follow-ups (improved or new versions) or other profitable products, have a limited future.

chapter 5

MARKET ANALYSIS SUMMARY

The *Market Analysis section*, or Industry Overview, comprises a summary of research concluding that your business idea is profitable. This section, when combined with your marketing strategy, which will be discussed in the next chapter, is considered the marketing plan. Marketing plans are often prepared separate from a business plan and used for internal purposes. Combined with the financial data, these sections provide the real "meat and potatoes" of your business plan.

Marketing is more than just how to advertise your business. Marketing covers everything from prospective customers to your competition to your charitable activities. The marketing plan will define your industry, discuss trends, outline the needs you will fill, create a target customer, and examine your competitors' weak spots.

Your market analysis looks at such issues as industry, business-to-business, consumer lifestyle trends, competitive influences, economic conditions, and population characteristics that affect sales volume. Analysis is really a series of questions asked and answered through research.

Begin this portion of your business plan by discussing your industry along with the specific information on the segment within the industry that applies to your business. The business associations, federal and state departments of commerce, universities, and trade organizations can provide appropriate statistics on your industry.

Key Market Analysis Questions

1. Will your products be trendy?

2. Will people buy more or less of your products or services?

3. Will lifestyle changes affect your sales? For instance, will health concerns keep people away or bring them in?

4. Do you anticipate that your competition will increase or decrease (independents or chain businesses)?

5. How will an aging population affect your business?

6. Do economic forecasts suggest changes in spending volume and habits (total sales volume and sales per customer)?

7. What are the implications of service demands shifts (faster service, more personalized service, automated service)?

Discuss the long-term prospects for your industry as well as for the type of business. Address the potential social and economic changes that may affect your industry. For example, the aging of America is a significant demographic change. How will this affect your services? building design? location? décor?

Begin by analyzing the industry as a whole. In the next section, we will develop specific strategies to capitalize on the information we uncover.

MARKET RESEARCH

Before you present your industry findings, it is important to explain where you acquired your information and how you assimilated those facts into your business plan. Here are some useful sources of information.

Primary and Secondary Market Research

Primary research is created for a specific purpose and includes focus groups, qualitative surveys, and phone interviews. Collect this information after you have identified a specific area you need to study.

Methods for gathering primary information include:

1. Surveys — Asking consumers a question directly.

2. Focus groups — Six to ten consumers are questioned in a discussion format.

3. Mail questionnaire — Used for extensive questioning to allow respondents to complete at their convenience.

4. Telephone surveys — Fast

and effective means of reaching a large group of people.

5. Observation — Watch people and try to learn what they do naturally.

Secondary research is research that has already been conducted for other purposes. It is found in sources like the Internet, books, and periodicals.

Tips for finding, and sources of, secondary information:

1. Search the Internet for "industry research reports."

2. Check your competitors' Web sites.

3. Dun and Bradstreet collect demographic and competitive information. Their reports can be attained for a fee at **www.dnb.com/us**.

4. Subscribe to industry newsletters.

5. Purchase the *Small Business Source Book* published by Gale Research.

6. Forrester Research (**www.forrester.com**) and Gartner Research (**www.gartner.com/Init**) publish detailed reports and studies focusing on the information technology industry.

7. Research demographics at the American Demographics Magazine (**www.adage.com/section.cms?sectionId=195**).

8. Federal and state governments publish reports on specific industries, markets, and products.

9. The U.S. Department of Commerce (**www.commerce.gov**) publishes the *U.S. Industrial Outlook* each January.

10. The U.S. Census Bureau (**www.census.gov**) publishes more than 100 current industrial reports on 5,000 manufactured products.

11. Consumer Information Reports provides specific information on production, shipping, inventories, consumption, and manufacturing firms per product.

12. Contact your local chamber of commerce.

13. Information from a wide variety of government sources may be found at **www.business.gov**.

Excerpt Alert

Market Research

To fully understand the market that Advanced Business Solutions is targeting, J. Jaxson talked to local businesses, consulted the Morrison Area Community Development Strategic Action Plan, joined the Chamber of Commerce, and researched Web-based consulting opportunities. She also surveyed companies within nearby communities to determine what services they offer and what fees they charge. Local business statistics as well as industry statistics from government sources were collected and analyzed, and J. Jaxson kept apprised of local issues affecting community businesses.

INDUSTRY ANALYSIS

In this section, you will define and describe the industry in which your business operates. The best way to start thinking about your industry and its particular issues is with a PEST analysis.

PEST Analysis

A PEST analysis looks at the Political, Economic, Social, and Technological drivers of a particular industry. PEST factors are external to your business and need to be understood when analyzing the industry as a whole. Depending on the market you are looking at, you may want to include Ecological and Legislative factors as well. Essentially, a PEST analysis measures the market potential by indicating areas of growth and decline.

PEST Analysis Framework

Political Factors	Economic Factors
• Ecological and environmental issues • Legislation—current and future • International legislation • Regulatory bodies and processes • Government policies • Government term and change • Funding, grants, initiatives • Lobby groups	• Domestic economy (situation and trends) • International situations and trends • Taxation issues • Seasonal issues • Market and trade cycles • Distribution issues • Interest and exchange rates
Social Factors	**Technological Factors**
• Lifestyle trends • Demographics • Consumer attitudes, opinions • Media views • Brand, company, technology image • Consumer buying patterns • Fashion and role models • Major events and influences • Ethnic and religious factors • Advertising and publicity	• Competing technology development • Associated and dependent technologies • Replacement technology and solutions • Maturity of technology • Information and communications • Technology legislation • Innovation potential • Technology access, licensing, patents • Intellectual property issues

Excerpt Alert

Size of the Industry

Management consulting is a dynamic and growing industry that not only generates significant revenues and profits, but also provides value to all types of organizations. Approximately 70 percent of all business and government organizations in the Okanagan area have used the services of a management consultant at least once in the past five years (Management Consulting Services, Industry Sector Analysis, 2002). The industry, which includes highly specialized sole practitioners; small- and medium-sized niche practices; and large, multinational firms, adds value to organizations of all sizes in the Okanagan area.

Management consulting in the Okanagan area is supported by a strong industry association, the Association of Management Consultants (AMC), which administers exams leading to the internationally recognized Certified Management Consultant (CMC) designation. Members adhere to a strict Code of Professional Conduct and work for firms of all sizes. J. Jaxson is a new member of this association.

Okanagan statistics show employment in this occupation is projected to grow much faster than the average for all occupations. Projections call for 4,170 openings to become available between 1998 and 2008. The technological revolution and the trend toward globalization have forced many businesses to hire business consultants in order to help them stay competitive within the rapidly changing business climate. Increasingly, traditional hardware, software, and telecommunications companies are opening consulting divisions. In addition, other professional service firms, such as law firms and advertising agencies, are beginning to provide management consulting services to their clients. These factors are expected to drive the growth of this occupational group through 2008.

This high growth can be partially attributed to the increasing reliance of large companies and governments on these professionals to provide them with analytical and advisory services that replace specialist and middle management staff. Businesses often find it more cost effective to hire independent consultants. There is lower overhead because a consultant can be contracted for work on specific tasks and removed from the payroll once the task has been completed.

Consulting revenue in the Okanagan area is concentrated in the most populous areas, with more than half of all revenue from Walton.

Distribution of Consulting Revenue in the Okanagan Area

	Total Revenue	% Total Okanagan
Walton	$2,935,726	51.2%
Haven	$1,160,266	20.2%
Morrison	$710,579	12.4%
Cadence	$629,197	11.0%
Masinet	$109,953	1.9%
Scheville	$64,971	1.1%
New Haven	$55,348	1.0%

	Total Revenue	% Total Okanagan
Normandy	$39,472	0.7%
Yorkville	$14,539	0.3%
Riverside	$9,543	0.2%
Tualameen	$6,429	0.1%
Okanagan	$5,736,024	

*Source: 2001 Survey of Service Industries:
Management, Scientific & Technical Consulting*

Morrison consultants account for 12.4 percent of the total Okanagan consulting revenue, and most of that is generated in the Lower Mainland area.

Employment by Area
Business Management Consultants
All Occupations

Lower Mainland	57%	77%
Hewitt	13%	18%
Granger	3%	10%
Morrison	7%	15%

*Work Futures Occupational Outlooks
updated November 1, 2000.*

Many of the largest firms have offices in at least one or two of the larger cities in the region. In the last few years, the accounting-based consulting firms have reduced the number of offices by exiting smaller communities. This has created a surge in the number of self-employed consultants and supports the opportunity created for self-employed consultants in communities not serviced by these large corporations.

Self-Employment

Management Consulting	51%
All Occupations	15%

Work Futures Occupational Outlooks last updated November 1, 2000.

Morrison is not currently served by any general management consulting firms; however, there are accounting firms in Morrison and outlying areas that offer management consulting services. Most consulting firms have developed their own market niches. Firms tend to become well known and recognized for their skills in a specific area such as organizational re-engineering, marketing, training, employee benefits, government program evaluation, or in a specific industry such as forestry, hospitality, health care, information technology, or communications. In Morrison, there are consulting firms that specialize in one specific area, such as hospitality, or one industry, such as forestry.

MARKET SEGMENTATION

Now that you have analyzed the industry as a whole, you need to break the entire market into the segments that are applicable to your venture. Highlight the segments you are targeting, and explain how these markets have evolved and are segmented (in terms of price, quality, channel of distribution, etc.). Indicate how and why the markets and key segments will develop over the life of your plan.

The process of segmentation helps you target

specific people with specific messages. In addition, segmentation helps you focus on the end-users' needs. In business as in life, you can't be all things to all people. Focus and concentrate on providing the best product or service for your target customer. Knowing your market segments will help you decide not only on which segment you should focus, but also on how to reach the customers within that segment.

Segmentation Factors

Business	Consumers
• Industry by SIC code	• Geographic location
• Size—revenue, number of employees	• Demographics/culture/religion
• Language	• Gender
• Status in the industry	• Age
• Future potential	• Social status
• Ability to make a quick purchase decision	• Education
• Access (or lack of access) to competitive offerings	• Special interests
• Need for customization	• Access (or lack of access) to competitive offerings
• Product or service application to a business function	• Need for specific information
	• Need for customization
	• Need for quality, durability, etc.

Provide information in your business plan that supports why you chose the particular segment of the market you are targeting.

Excerpt Alert

Key Product Segments

Consulting and communications are diverse industries. There are hundreds of different services that consultants provide to all industries and industry sectors.

Management Consulting — Client Base as Percent of Total Revenue

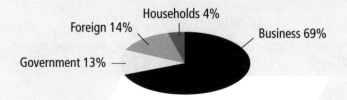

The key markets for consulting services are corporations; municipal, regional, provincial, and federal governments; foreign businesses; and households.

Key Market Segments

Key market segments vary by consulting specialty. The services offered by consulting companies are divided into the following main categories:

- Strategy and Organization
- Financial
- Project Management
- Human Resources and Search
- Change Management
- Marketing
- Operations Management
- Process Re-engineering, Facilities/Outsourcing
- Other

Leading Okanagan Consultancies: Fee Split by Activity

	IT	Strategy & Organization	Financial	Project Mgmt	HR & Search	Change Mgmt	Marketing	Operations Mgmt	Process Re-engineering	Facilities / Outsourcing	Others
Ajilon	20	15		5	27	10	3		10	10	
Aon Consulting					14					86	
Computer Sciences Corporation	30	20	20			10		10	10		
Hay Management Consultants		15			80	5					
KPMG Consulting	30	8	0.5	7	29	2	0.5		21	1	1
Pricewaterhouse Coopers	60	10								30	

Source: Management Consultant International: January 20, 2000.

Use simple tables and charts to illustrate key points and to drill down into the appropriate detail.

MARKET TRENDS AND OUTLOOK

This section explains what is going on in your market. What trends or fashions are influencing the market segment(s) you have identified? Discuss product and technology trends, and indicate the likely impact of changes in the factors you identified in your PEST analysis. You must be aware of the trends that will affect the ability of your business to achieve and maintain profitability.

Read the newspaper and publications produced by businesses in your area to spot key trends and to get a sense of the general outlook. Much of the information gathered in this section comes from observing what is going on around you, and then applying it to your business situation. After surveying the trends that are applicable to your market, summarize your findings in your business plan.

Excerpt Alert

Key Industry Trends

The consulting industry is growing for two key reasons. One is that demand for consulting services is increasing as companies downsize and contract out work that was historically done in-house. Corporate downsizing has also resulted in many managers being laid off. It is difficult for many of these people to find similar employment, and as a result, many of these managers start their own businesses. Approximately 10 percent become consultants, many providing consulting services to the firms they just left. Those who start other types of businesses may require specialized consulting services to improve their chances of success. Therefore, corporate downsizing has resulted in an increase both in the supply of and in the demand for consulting services.

Consulting has risen 10 percent annually over the last several years. Approximately 100 new businesses were started in the area. This trend is projected to continue for at least another five years.

Industry Outlook

With the continued economic and political uncertainty in this region, the demand for consulting services will grow as many companies are reluctant to hire additional employees. More and more work will be contracted to outside consultants as companies maintain tight control over labor costs. This trend is also true in the government sector, which is under increasing pressure to lower costs by reducing employment levels. Although the number of business starts has increased, so has the number of bankruptcies. Approximately seven out of ten new businesses will fail within the first two years of operation, primarily due to poor management. Some people who start new businesses lack basic business skills. The demand for small business training and assistance will grow as these entrepreneurs seek the assistance they require in order to reduce their risk of business failure.

The Morrison Area Community Development Strategic Action Plan states "a lack of business skills in upper and middle management limits business development..." and as one of the projects to increase skills in existing business, it recommends "business skills training for management." This indicates an interest in and commitment to professional business management, fitting nicely with the services provided by Advanced Business Solutions.

INDUSTRY PARTICIPANTS

Here you will describe the main characteristics of the firms that operate within the market segment you are targeting. Common variables used to describe industry participants include:

- Revenue

- Number of employees

- Region

- Urban or rural setting

- Payroll earnings

- Average annual earnings

- Number of businesses

- Sales

- Profits

- Balance sheet data (assets, liabilities, equity)

- Income

Excerpt Alert

Description of Industry Participants

As described earlier, 51 percent of management consultants are self-employed. The remaining consultants work at firms that are divided into large firms with more than 100 employees, medium-sized firms with 20 to 100 employees, and small firms with fewer than 20 employees. The majority (66 percent) of these consultants in Okanagan are employed at large firms, 6 percent at medium-sized firms, and 28 percent at small firms, according to a recent industry report. The large consulting firms are usually U.S.-based firms, including Andersen Consulting, Deloitte & Touche, Ernst & Young, KPMG, and PricewaterhouseCoopers. Small firms typically have fewer than ten employees.

Where Consultants Work,
By Firm Size

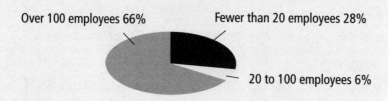

Over 100 employees 66%   Fewer than 20 employees 28%

20 to 100 employees 6%

Source: Industry Profile, Management Consulting Services

PURCHASE PROCESSES/BUYING PATTERNS

In this section, you answer the question, "How do consumers purchase the product or service you intend to sell?"

Consumer buying behavior is the way in which people go about making a decision to purchase a product or service. When analyzing your market, you need to understand:

- Why consumers make the purchases that they make.

- What factors influence consumer purchases.

Consumer buying behavior is influenced by the amount of risk inherent in the purchase: the greater the risk, the more involvement in the purchase. There's not much risk involved in buying a stick of deodorant, so not a lot of thought goes into the purchase. On the other hand, the purchase of a car involves a great deal of risk, so the amount of preparation and planning increases accordingly.

Factors that affect the consumer buying process are categorized in three ways, include the following:

Factors Affecting Consumer Buying

Personal Factors	Psychological Factors	Social Factors
• Demographic factors—sex, race, age, etc. • Who is responsible for the decision making	• Motives • Perception • Ability and knowledge • Attitudes • Personality • Lifestyles	• Opinion leaders • Roles and family influences • Reference groups • Social class • Culture and sub-culture

If your business is marketing to the business consumer, you must think about other factors as well. The industrial market consists of fewer buyers, larger buyers, and more geographically concentrated buyers. The demand is less elastic, and it fluctuates more with overall economic factors. The purchasing process is much more professional, and there are more buying influences involved. When you market to this group, you must determine:

- Who the major participants in the buying process are.

- Which decisions each participant influences.

- What each participant's relative degree of influence is.

- What evaluation criteria each participant will use.

Think about the factors that will affect your targeted customers, and summarize your findings in your business plan.

Excerpt Alert

Purchase Process and Buying Criteria

The buying process for consulting and communications services varies by type of client and service. Businesses find and choose consulting firms using several methods.

Referral

Businesses find consultants through their lending institutions, business or industry associations, friends or colleagues, and the telephone directory. Businesses contact these consulting firms to obtain proposals and price quotes for the required services. A consulting firm is chosen based on such needs of the client as price and quality of proposal, as well as the reputation, past experience, and level of expertise of the consulting firm.

Request for Proposal

Government and other businesses requiring consulting services sometimes distribute a "Request for Proposal" to a number of consulting firms that they would like to bid on a specific project. These consulting firms submit proposals for the projects outlining the scope of the work, the methodology, a work plan, and a price quote. These proposals are evaluated based on criteria developed by the client. The proposal evaluation criteria varies by project and client but usually includes price and quality of proposal, and the reputation, past experience, and level of expertise of the consulting firm.

Online Bidding Through Service-Procurement Sites

Consultants register or pay a fee to subscribe to a procurement site. They then have access to bid on any of the jobs posted by companies using the site to solicit consultation services. The winning bidder is selected by the company based on price, experience, quality of proposal, and work samples provided. The work is then conducted via electronic communication.

MISTAKES TO AVOID

- **Not doing your homework.** Be well informed on the companies within your industry, and know how your business will fit in.

- **Incomplete analysis.** Do not overlook national industry data that can be a predictor of business cycles, buying patterns, and growth potential.

chapter 6

MARKET STRATEGY

Your marketing strategy is the obvious extension of the analysis you finished in the previous section. Your marketing strategy explains the "how" and the "who" aspects of your business proposition. **How will you market/sell your product or service, and to whom?**

By now you have a pretty good idea of what your marketing focus will be, but to further refine it, complete a SWOT analysis. A SWOT analysis looks at the Strengths, Weaknesses, Opportunities and Threats facing your business idea and the market in which it operates.

Strength — Internal factor that contributes to a company's profitability.

Weakness — Internal factor that decreases a company's profitability.

Opportunity — An area of need in which a company can perform profitably.

Threat — A challenge posed by an unfavorable trend or development that could lead to profit deterioration.

SWOT Analysis Framework

Strengths	Weaknesses
• Distinct capabilities	• Gaps in capabilities
• Competitive advantages	• Lack of competitive strength
• Resources (including people)	• Reputation, presence, reach
• Experience, knowledge, data	• Financials
• Financial reserves, likely returns	• Vulnerabilities
• Innovative aspects	• Deadlines and pressures
• Location	• Cash flow and cash drain
• Price, value, quality	• Reliability of data, plan predictability
• Accreditations	• Morale, commitment, leadership
• IT	

Opportunities	Threats
• Market developments	• Politics
• Competitors' vulnerabilities	• Legislation
• Industry and lifestyle trends	• Environment
• Technology development and innovation	• IT developments
• International changes	• Competitor intentions
• New markets	• Market demand
• Business and product development	• New technologies, services, ideas
• Information and research	• Loss of key staff
• Partnerships, agencies, distribution	• Finances
• Scale efficiencies	• Economy

By completing this analysis, you will have an excellent idea of how you can align your strengths with the opportunities available, and you can prepare contingencies for dealing with identified weaknesses and industry threats.

With this information, you can develop not only the marketing strategy portion of your business plan but also a blueprint to follow when you begin operations.

TARGET MARKETS

You have broken your industry into market segments, and now you must decide which segments to target. Your evaluation criteria are:

- Segment size and growth — Does the segment offer enough opportunity in terms of quantity?

- Segment structural attractiveness — What are the forces (substitute products, new entrants, supplier and buyer power) that are working within the segment to undermine profitability ?

- Company objectives and resources — Does the segment fit with the overall company mission and values?

Your Customers

Without paying customers, there is no reason to open your doors. A powerful tool in developing your marketing concept is to create a customer profile based upon geographic, demographic, and economic data, combined with personal observations. By defining your ideal customer, you'll have a mental image on which to build your business. You'll know whom you should talk to in your advertising, the type of décor that would attract him or her, and the service he or she would like to find in your business.

By "ideal" customer, I am referring to an imaginary person who will like your business, appreciate your products, and return frequently. Looking at the population in your community will help you define this person (or persons) by average age, economic status, gender, family size, transportation method, and more.

Examples of target customers

- Your target "after work" bar patron might be a young professional, most likely male, with an above-average income, who drives a sports car, and is a sharp dresser who dines out three or four nights a week.

- Your target fast-food customer might be young or single-parent families with children under the age of 12, rushing home after work, needing a fast to-go meal at value pricing to be consumed at home.

- Your typical fitness club member might be female, 22 to 45, an elegant casual dresser, who doesn't have time for a full-hour training session.

- Your desired men's wear customer is vacationing at a nearby resort area, who dresses according to season (skiwear or sun wear), and is interested in high-end, name-brand clothing in natural materials.

Customer Demographics

An efficient way to identify your ideal target customer is with the following demographic data:

- Affluence—Discretionary income for necessities and luxuries

- Age

- Marital status

- Family size—Number of adults and children per family

- Gender

- Ethnicity—Cultural habits and expectations

- Sexual orientation

- Education levels

- Local wages

- Seasonal or stable population—Tourist influx, volume cycles

Your Customers' Needs

Once you have identified a target customer, you must assess what customer needs your business will fill. For example, if you are opening a coffee shop or café that caters to the local theater crowd, then you are filling the need for late-dining choices.

Types of needs your business can fill:

- Physical — Shelter, food, transportation

- Emotional — Comfort, creativity, nostalgia

- Convenience — Easy to buy, minimal hassles

- Financial — Pricing that fits customers' perceived value and/or budget

- Stress-relief — Provides enjoyment while making life easier for customers juggling multiple demands

- Pleasure — Entertainment, comfortable surroundings, products and services that "reward" people, enhanced looks, vanity

- Attention — A way to demonstrate class or wealth, to see and be seen by others

- Fellowship — A place for people to meet, to share conversations, a dating destination

- Protection—Security, peace of mind, protection, immunity, safety, quality, nutritional value, warding off fear for self and family

Your Company's Solutions

The second half of the need/solution equation is how you will satisfy your customers' needs. These should be posed as "solutions." Below are some solution examples various businesses might use to target their customers' needs.

- Your restaurant serves food to satisfy your customers' hunger pangs. Fill their minds with delicious ways to fulfill their **physical** needs.

- Memories of smells, tastes, sights, and good times often trigger a need that must be satisfied. Trends often result from an effort to satisfy these **emotional** "cravings."

- **Convenience** can mean location, style of service, hours of operation and delivery service. Make it easy to purchase by accepting credit and debit cards.

- **Affordable** means different things to different people. Does your pricing fit in with the economic picture of your community? Affordable isn't always rock-bottom pricing.

It means *perceived value*. For some people, a $499 pair of shoes would be perfectly acceptable; while others would feel that they were being robbed! Is the price appropriate for the quality? Does your customer service add value to the customer's visit and increase the perceived value?

- Hungry kids, busy schedules, and frustrating traffic delays are all part of modern-day stress. Many buying decisions are made based on the **stress relief** they provide. Satisfying the needs of children is a powerful way to bring in families. McDonalds® created an empire by stimulating children's wants so that parents respond by choosing fast food for meals.

- **Pleasure** is a primary reason people spend money. Whether it is a cashmere sweater, a new set of golf clubs, or movie tickets, Americans buy things to reward themselves. Pleasure is a powerful motivator.

- **Attention** (vanity) is another major influence on purchasing decisions. People want to feel good about themselves and their appearance. Making clients feel pampered is a great way to appeal to consumers. Another is to appeal to the desire for social status — the "see-and-be-seen" factor.

- **Fellowship** offers customers another reason to visit your business. Social gatherings at restaurants, bars, amusement parks, and other businesses are a great way to connect. Think about providing families with an atmosphere in which they want to gather, celebrate special occasions, and mark important life events. A friendly environment and staff gives road-weary business travelers and lonely customers a chance to connect with others.

- **Fear** is a powerful motivator. It can be used directly, as in, "Anything else puts your family at risk." Using fear indirectly to market your products and services requires just a slight jab at "panic buttons." Providing a solution that *frees customers from fear* is a great way to tap virtually every market segment. Whether promoting pesticide-free ingredients or shorter stopping distances, your business frees clients from worry.

Niche Marketing

Knowing what sets your business apart can ensure that you capture your fair share of the market. Uniqueness is a great value to explore and include in the plan's Competition section. Describe what makes your business special. Do you have a specialty or an "entertainment" factor? Sometimes what sets you apart from your competition are such mundane attributes as longer hours, free parking, or "kids eat free" specials.

- Look for ways to set your business apart from the competition without resorting to such overused descriptions as "better quality" or "friendlier" service. People tend to ignore these.

- Look for areas that have been overlooked or underserved — the niche.

- Become a trusted expert in your niche through PR and advertising.

Excerpt Alert

Target Markets

Our target markets will include all businesses operating within Morrison as well as entrepreneurs pursuing business development. For the Web-based procurement sites, small business and individuals will be targeted, and we will also submit proposals in response to any Request for Proposal we receive as well as for any relevant provincial and federal government contracts.

MISTAKES TO AVOID

- **Not knowing your ideal customer.** Of course you'd like to sell to everyone in the community, but the truth is you'll have a select group of ideal customers that you focus your marketing toward.

- **Assuming everyone is a potential customer.** Your products and services may cross demographic categories, but you need to focus on the realities of who will need, want, and pay for your offerings. Everyone eats, but not everyone is interested in authentic Pakistani delicacies.

- **Overstating potential customer market size.** Sell to enough customers to be profitable with growth potential.

- **Working too many market segments.** Select the market segment (selling direct to the end-user, selling through a distributor, or selling direct to the reseller) that offers you the greatest success rate—don't try to sell to everyone.

KEY COMPETITORS

Rarely is there an idea that is without competitors vying for customers' dollars. Direct competitors can be either the businesses within a specific territory or those that offer the same products nation- or worldwide. However, an indirect competitor may not offer exactly what you do, but if potential customers could legitimately compare and contrast their products with your products and services, consider them as competition.

To fill out this section of your **FAST PLAN**, you'll need to compile a list of businesses that will have the greatest competitive effect on your company. Analyzing their strengths and weaknesses will give you insights into ways to outperform them and isolate a niche market (a specific customer need that isn't being well served). Your competitive analysis can also help you identify the marketing efforts you'll need to capture your share of the market.

Your research and analysis of the competition is critical to assessing your potential for success. You'll have to find paying customers in two ways: 1) by drawing in those who don't regularly buy your type of product or service, and 2) by taking customers away from your competition.

Competitor Analysis

1. Who are your five nearest direct competitors?

2. Who are your indirect competitors?

3. How are their businesses: steady? increasing? decreasing?

4. What have you learned from their operations? from their advertising?

5. What are their strengths and weaknesses?

6. How does their product or service differ from yours?

Create a file on each of the competitors identified in your analysis and keep track of how they:

- Advertise—When do they advertise? Where do they advertise?

- Promote—Do they sponsor events?

- Price—When do they run sales? What type of discounts do they offer?

Excerpt Alert

Description of Key Competitors

There are five accounting service providers in Morrison and another 19 firms advertising in the Salmon Arm/ Morrison Yellow Pages. Of these, only two consider themselves to provide management consulting beyond accounting, finance, and basic tax issues: BDO Dunwoody, with a location in Morrison, and KPMG in Vernon. BDO Dunwoody provides consulting services within the community; however, their presence in that field is not well known or advertised. They have three accountants working from the office and some students (working toward their CA), and thus do not have the breadth or depth of knowledge that Advanced Business Solutions brings to the consulting services offered. KPMG in Vernon specializes in accounting and finance but can access many consulting resources through their national network. These additional services are offered only to existing clients and on a limited basis, and it is not an area that is marketed at all.

There are four business or management consultants listed in the telephone directory, and of those, one deals strictly with accounting, one specializes in hospitality, one is no longer in service, and one offers human resource-related consulting but it is geared more to the relationship aspects of work (teamwork, employee assistance programs, mediation) than human resource system development. Other consultants in the area focus on employment, forestry, or other industry-specific areas, not general management consulting.

MISTAKES TO AVOID

- **"No competition" is not a good thing.** Most business ideas are already in existence. If you have no competition, it may be a signal that there is not a need, it is not a viable idea, or you cannot make a profit.

- **Underestimating the competition.** Every business has competition, and underestimating ability to compete with a new business can be costly.

- **Forgetting indirect competition.** An indirect competitor is an alternate choice for potential customers that may not look or act the way your business does. For example, ready-made salads in the local market are an indirect competitor of a salad-bar restaurant.

ANALYSIS OF COMPETITIVE POSITION

Taking the information gleaned from your target market definition and competitor analysis, write a summary analysis of your competitive position. Include information gathered from your marketing analysis as well as from the PEST and SWOT analyses to support your position and conclusions.

Excerpt Alert

Analysis of Competitive Position

Advanced Business Solutions will be the only consulting firm in the region with strong business credentials offering management consulting and specialized business solutions. Advanced Business Solutions has a competitive advantage in this area due to the superior combination of education with the management and consulting experience of J. Jaxson. J. Jaxson has a master's degree in Business Administration (MBA), is a Certified Human Resource Professional (CHRP), and has more than five years of management and consulting experience within Morrison.

As a new business, it may take time to establish a strong client base and develop a reputation as a business solutions expert; however, J. Jaxson already has proven her abilities in a number of high-profile local arenas. She taught business and computer courses at the local chapter of the Okanagan University College, she managed the HR function at the water bottling plant, she has provided workshops for the local Skills Center, and she has performed limited business consultation while developing the concept of Advanced Business Solutions.

Word-of-mouth is the most important type of advertising there is, and in a small community like Morrison, reputation is everything. J. Jaxson has been assured by many former business associates that they will highly recommend her services to anyone who inquires.

PRICING STRATEGY

Setting appropriate prices requires a combination of financial analysis, competitive research, and demographic data. So how much should you charge? Will your customers be able to afford $100 golf shirts, or will they prefer lower-priced polos? Your pricing strategy can be used to improve your overall competitiveness, but it should be in line with your competition as well as with industry averages.

Your pricing strategy is closely tied to your financial projections and therefore needs to be accurate. You must know your ingredient and material costs and overhead figures. In addition, you must have completed a break-even analysis.

 Break-Even Analysis

A break-even analysis lets you determine what you need to sell to cover your costs of doing business. It is the point at which you achieve a zero profit.

1. To start a break-even analysis you must break down your costs into fixed and variable.

    Fixed costs do not change based on sales volume (rent, insurance).

    Variable costs change based on sales volume (raw materials, labor).

2. Calculate your variable costs as a percentage of total sales:

   Variable Costs = 50,000

   Total Sales = 175,000

   Variable Cost % = 50,000/175,000 = 28.6%

3. Perform a break-even (BE) analysis:

   Break-Even Sales = Fixed Costs + (Variable Cost % * Sales)

Typically, you will use your direct competitors' pricing strategies as a guide from which to start and then modify your pricing model to reflect your unique selling proposition.

Common Pricing Strategies

- Retail cost and pricing

- Competitive position

- Pricing below competition

- Pricing above competition

- Price lining

- Multiple pricing

- Service costs and pricing (for service businesses only)

    — Service components

    — Material costs

    — Labor costs

    — Overhead costs

Excerpt Alert

Pricing Strategy

Advanced Business Solutions' services will be priced competitively with other small consulting firms. Typically, the fees charged by small firms that have much lower overhead costs are much lower than those charged by the large firms. Advanced Business Solutions' fees will be based on several factors including the time and resources needed to complete a project, overhead costs, and the fees charged by other competitive consulting firms. Hourly rates will range from $45 to $60. Large firms typically charge an average of $250 per hour, and the local office of BDO Dunwoody has rates that range from $50 per hour for consulting provided by a student to $300 per hour for the most qualified CA working on a complex issue.

Fair market value would suggest we charge at least $75 per hour; however, the majority (65.5 percent) of Morrison businesses have a payroll of less than $75,000, and only 8 percent have a payroll over $350,000, indicating that clients will be price-sensitive. As a start-up business, we need to build a client base and encourage local businesses to engage our services, thus we have to be careful not to price ourselves out of the market before we have an opportunity to prove our value to the community.

Our hourly fees will vary depending on the nature of the work but will not be determined by the ability of the firm to pay. Total project costs will vary depending on the time needed to complete the project as well as the direct expenses incurred as part of the project.

MISTAKES TO AVOID

- **Equating a lower price with sales potential.** Undercutting the competition isn't necessarily a way to capture customers from the competition.

PROMOTION STRATEGY

How you advertise and promote your goods and services may make or break your business. Advertising and PR are critical to attracting customers. How will you let your potential customers know about your business? What types of paid advertising will you implement and what results do you expect? How will PR be handled?

Your advertising needs (and budget) are affected

by your competitors' activities, your location, and your local customers. Advertising has two primary functions. The first is to bring in paying customers, while the second is to develop a brand name for your business for long-term sales.

Bringing in people now should be your number-one goal with all advertising and public relations campaigns. In your early days, you'll need to keep the cash flow consistent to take care of expenses. However, you'll also need to commit, from day one, a percentage of your advertising budget to long-term brand building.

Your initial advertising efforts should concentrate on reaching potential customers within your

neighborhood. Start with a sign announcing your arrival the day you sign the lease or break ground. Begin the buzz early with the media. Plan a community-wide grand opening, inviting suppliers and others who helped launch your business, and advertise it at least two weeks in advance.

To write the Marketing section and establish a preliminary budget, explore the various types of advertising and public relations efforts available in your community. From billboards to Web sites, there are dozens of ways to tell your story and bring in customers.

The most effective advertising is the one that most frequently reaches your desired target audience. If your target audience is comprised of high school and college students, don't advertise in the local business journal. If your business is a perfect gathering spot for dinner meetings, place an appropriate ad in local business publications.

Remember that advertising is an investment that takes time before you see a return. Create campaigns in multiple venues that are seen repeatedly by prospective customers. Don't give up if nothing seems to be happening the first week. Advertising gurus advise patience, as it can take up to seven exposures to an ad before someone takes action.

Don't be passive in your advertising. Be a little bossy! Tell people what you want them to do. "Stop by and try our juicy cheeseburgers with hand-cut fries" or "Call today and ..."

Word-of-mouth advertising will develop naturally, but it is a slow process. You can accelerate it by promoting loyalty, encouraging people to refer you, and spending as much money on keeping your customers as you do on acquiring new ones!

Business reviews are also word-of-mouth advertising. Business and community reporters like to visit the new spot in town. Do some dry runs and pre-opening events to get your staff up to speed before a reviewer visits.

Remember, too, that one of the most critical parts of developing ongoing advertising campaigns is your ability to measure its success. When people make appointments, ask how they heard about you. Leave a comment card at the table along with the check. Include a prepaid response postcard in the package. Build in measurable response mechanisms such as coupons or frequent-buyer card programs.

Advertising

When thinking about advertising, consider where your ideal customer would most likely hear about you. Match your advertising to their habits. Concentrate on advertising methods that are closest to where your customers live and work. A huge freeway billboard is a real eye-catcher, but will it bring business to an establishment that is located 15 miles north?

To learn more about small business advertising, check out Jay Conrad Levinson at **www.gmarketing.com**. His advice and practical "guerilla marketing" philosophy are aimed at small businesses interested in maximizing their marketing efforts without breaking their budgets. He has authored several books on practical and affordable public relations and advertising.

Additional resources on small business advertising can be found in Chapter 12 – *Business Plan References*.

Branding

The process of creating a recognition factor for your business is called branding. Branding your business starts with finding a name that connects with customers. The name might be something very chic like "Noir," homey like "Mama Rosa's," silly like "Peter Piper's Pickled Peppers," or whimsical like "Mr. Mouse's House." The business name you select should reflect the overall image you are trying to create.

If your legal name is different from your business name, you'll need to file an assumed business name (also know as a DBA or "doing business as") with your local governing authority. Check with city, county, and state agencies governing new businesses, and comply with their specific requirements. In addition, consider registering the name and logo as trademarks. The U.S. Patent and Trademark Office has information available at **www.uspto.gov**. Check out the article on small business trademarks at ABC Small Biz at **www. abcsmallbiz.com/bizbasics/gettingstarted/ trademark.html**.

Along with your business brand name, you'll need a logo and color scheme to create a consistent message and appearance. Consistency is important in the branding process. Think of the brown UPS® trucks and uniforms or the bright Coca-Cola® red that has remained the same over the decades. An inconsistent image is one of the most common mistakes a new business makes.

Promotional Mix

A promotional mix is an allocation of resources among five primary elements:

Promotion	Advantages	Disadvantages

ADVERTISING
• Print ads
• Radio TV
• Billboards
• Web advertising
  - Banner ads
  - Paid listings
  - Pay-per-click
    links
  - Pay-per-sale
    advertising
  - "Opt-in" e-mail
    advertising
	• Credibility
	• Timing
	• Drama
	• Branding
		• Cost
		• Follow through
		• Lack of feedback
		• Consumer
		  indifference

DIRECT MARKETING
• Catalogs
• Coupon mailers
• Letters
	• Predictability
	• Effectiveness in
	  reaching the right
	  target
	• Ease of
	  measurement
		• Saturation
		• Reliance on
		  obsolete direct-
		  mail lists
		• Heightened need
		  for customer
		  service

Promotion	Advantages	Disadvantages
SALES PROMOTION • In-store demonstrations • Displays • Contests • Price incentives	• Build relationships • Stir excitement • Gauge price sensitivity	• Risk of misfire • Risk of dependency • Risk of trivializing your brand
PUBLIC RELATIONS • Hosting special events • Sponsoring charitable campaigns	• Believability • Employee morale • Educating visitors	• Cost • Lack of control • Failure to hit target
PERSONAL SELLING • Door-to-door selling	• Clear message • Gauge consumer response	• Intrusive • Cost

Excerpt Alert

Promotion Strategy

Advanced Business Solutions will market its services by listing with all local business and industry associations; advertising in the local newspapers; placing an ad in the telephone directory; developing an introductory flyer to be sent to all chamber of commerce members; sending a detailed business package to key businesses, the City of Morrison, business and development associations, and local government offices; networking with the local business community; and becoming an active member of business and consulting associations.

Introductory Flyer and Business Package

A one-page flyer will be produced and distributed to all Morrison Chamber of Commerce members. This flyer will quickly summarize the services offered and invite businesses to call to discuss how we can work together to achieve their operational goals.

A detailed business package will then be sent to lending institutions, associations, key business leaders, and potential clients, outlining J. Jaxson's experience, qualifications, and level of expertise, as well as a comprehensive list of services available and a convincing set of reasons why they should engage Advanced Business Solutions' services

Advertising

We will place an ad in both local newspapers. The *Times Review* has a variety of ways to advertise, including business profiles. We will advertise selectively within a limited budget. Within the next two years, we will develop our own Internet site, highlighting our expertise and services.

Advanced Business Solutions will also place an ad in the local telephone directory.

Networking

Advanced Business Solutions will join local business associations in order to maintain contacts in the business community as well as to stay well informed about the issues that are important to local businesses.

Advanced Business Solutions will join the Human Resource Management Association (HRMA) and the Association of Management Consultants (AMC) to maintain professional credentials and keep abreast of important issues facing the industry.

MISTAKES TO AVOID

- **Underestimating the cost of advertising.** In some industries, advertising costs can exceed the cost of raw materials. You cannot assume the product will "sell itself"; you must be prepared to introduce, support, and continually tell people about your products, services, and company.

chapter 7

MANAGEMENT SUMMARY

Managing a business requires more than just
the desire to be your own boss. It demands
dedication, persistence, the capacity to make
wise decisions, and the ability to manage both employees
and finances. Your Management Summary, along with
your Marketing and Financial Management sections, is
your business foundation.

Take a good look at the talents you possess and the skills
you lack. Your job is to hire personnel who can supply
your "missing" skills. Staff are your greatest business
resource and most valuable asset — spend their energy

wisely, respect them, and reward them to build a strong team.

You also need to look at how you can best serve your business. Even if you can create a P&L statement or design a Web page, consider if this is the best use of your time. First, you'll need to invest your time in activities that earn money. If you are the creative talent in the business, don't hesitate to outsource or hire someone to handle the operational and support duties. Learn to train people for advancement and to delegate duties. Entrepreneurs often like to "do it themselves," feel they are the "only one who can do it," or think they cannot afford outside help. This is a self-limited managerial style. Share the duties and responsibilities, and you'll have rewards to share also.

Your management plan should answer such questions as:

1. How does your background and business experience help in this business?

2. Who will be on the management team?

3. What are your weaknesses and how can you compensate for them? (Although you won't write directly about the weak spots, they will be noticed by business professionals. Explain the "missing" skills before someone can question your team's ability.)

4. What are the team's strengths and weaknesses?

5. What are their duties? Are these duties clearly defined?

6. If a franchise, what type of assistance can you expect from the franchisor? Will this assistance be ongoing?

7. What are your current personnel needs?

8. What are your plans for hiring and training personnel?

9. What salaries, benefits, vacations, and holidays will you offer?

10. If a franchise, are these issues covered in the management package the franchisor will provide?

11. How will you attract quality employees? How can do you plan to enhance productivity?

12. What benefits, if any, can you afford at this point?

If this is a franchise, the operating procedures, manuals, and materials devised by the franchisor should be included in this section of the business plan. (If they are too bulky, simply list them by title and refer the reader to their location.) Lenders can consider the strength of the franchisor as part of your management capabilities. Study these documents carefully when writing your business plan, and be sure to incorporate the important highlights. The franchisor should assist you with management training and ongoing management support.

YOUR KEY PERSONNEL

As the owner/operator of a small business, you'll probably hold all the key positions in your company — owner, employee, accountant, personnel director. Tell the reader what makes you capable of filling these roles.

- If your business requires support staff, look for experienced personnel to share the responsibility of daily operations, decision making, and supervision of people and resources. Here is where you will discuss the skills and expertise your key personnel bring to your business.

Outside Support

An owner or manager need not handle all of the business's fiscal and managerial responsibilities. Outside consultants and advisors are a great way to enhance your management resources. Your accountant, lawyer, insurance broker, ad agency, PR firm, remodeling contractor, real estate broker, business equipment salesperson, and suppliers can add depth to your management capabilities.

Management Philosophy

Your management style indicates how you make decisions, how you delegate, and how you interact with personnel. Discuss your team-building philosophy and other work ethics that support your mission statement.

Organizational Chart

Depending upon the size of your organization, you can either include a chart or simply describe who will report to whom. Organizational or flow charts can be created using the chart and diagram functions of Microsoft Word and Excel.

Excerpt Alert

Organizational Structure

Advanced Business Solutions is a sole proprietorship that will be run and managed by the owner, J. Jaxson. All administrative duties, including bookkeeping, will be done by J. Jaxson, and accounting obligations for year-end will be contracted to an outside provider. Any additional staff required will be obtained on a subcontract basis.

Management Team

J. Jaxson is a Certified Human Resource Professional (CHRP) with a master's degree in Business Administration (MBA) and a bachelor's degree in Psychology. She is a member of the Beta Gamma Sigma honors society for business graduates. She belongs to two professional associations: the Human Resource Management Association (HRMA) and the Association of Management Consultants (AMC).

J. Jaxson's résumé is attached at the end of this business plan.

Staffing

No full-time staff will be hired at Advanced Business Solutions for at least three years. Any additional staff required to complete client contracts will be hired on a subcontract basis in order to keep labor costs low.

chapter 8

FINANCIAL PLAN

It *is possible to be* a successful businessperson
without being an accounting wizard. The key is to hire
a good bookkeeper for daily tasks and an accountant
for monthly, quarterly, and annual financial reports and
tax obligations. You can pay people to do the number
crunching, but you must know how to read and use the
information in these reports. Your business's accounting
is not just something you do to please the IRS; it is your
guide to profitability.

In the Financial section, you will transform your wish
lists, budgets, and assumptions into financial reports.
A significant portion of your first projections will be

conjecture. The goal is to analyze and determine at what levels you will begin to become profitable, whether you have sufficient starting and working capital, and whether your profit potential is worth your time and money investment.

During this process, you'll calculate how much money you need in addition to your personal investment. In order to qualify for a loan or investment, you must also be able to prove your ability to repay the loan or give an investor an appropriate return.

Hiring an accountant with industry-specific (retail, manufacturing, service) experience can be a wise move. He or she will understand your business cycle as well as the tax laws that apply to your specific business. In addition, an accountant will be able to help you determine ways to improve your financial outlook.

Sound financial management ensures your business will remain profitable and solvent. It is the cornerstone of every successful business venture. Each year businesses with significant sales numbers fail because of poor or inadequate financial management. As a business owner, you will need to identify and implement policies that ensure you can meet your financial obligations.

To effectively manage your finances, plan a sound,

realistic budget by determining the actual amount of money needed to open your business (start-up costs) and the amount needed to keep it open (operating costs). The first step to building a sound financial plan is to devise a start-up budget. Your start-up budget will usually include such one-time-only costs as major equipment, utility deposits, and down payments.

The Financial section of your business plan should include any loan applications filed, capital equipment and supply list, balance sheet, break-even analysis, pro-forma income projections (profit and loss statement), and pro-forma cash flow projections. The income statement and cash flow projections should include a three-year summary (detail by month for the first year, then by quarter for the second and third years).

Developing projections is probably the most difficult aspect of writing your business plan. Strive to be as accurate as possible based upon your research. Overstating your sales in hopes of impressing lenders or investors can backfire. Understating your sales can mean that you won't be prepared to satisfy the demand.

The accounting system (including sales and inventory management) along with your fiscal calendar dates are also addressed in this section of the business plan.

STARTING-OUT NEEDS

Your start-up capital must cover everything from the business license to telephone company deposits to stocking the shelves. Investigate these thoroughly as they can add up quickly.

Document your sources of available cash, outlining your assumptions on calculating specific estimated expenses. For example, raw materials and cost of goods sold may rely on good-faith estimates based upon your business and industry experience. Final pricing negotiations take time or fluctuate wildly.

If start-up costs don't exceed available cash, explain how the balance will be used. If you are still seeking additional financing, weigh this use against upcoming needs. If start-up costs are greater than available cash, you'll need to discuss where you'll secure balance, whether it be a combination of personal investment, loans, or outside investment.

OPERATING BUDGET

An operating budget is prepared when you are ready to open for business. The operating budget will reflect your priorities in terms of how you spend your money, the expenses you will incur, and how you will meet those expenses (income). The operating budget will include additional investment or loans necessary to cover the first six to nine months of operation.

If a franchise, the franchisor may stipulate in the franchise contract the type of accounting and inventory systems you may use. If this is the case, he or she may have a system available for your use. Whether you develop the accounting and inventory systems yourself, have an outside financial advisor develop the systems, or the franchisor provides these systems, you will need to acquire a thorough understanding of each segment and how it operates. Your financial advisor can assist you in developing this section of your business plan.

The following questions should help you determine the amount of start-up capital you will need to purchase and open a franchise.

- How much money do you have?

- How much money will you need to purchase the franchise?

- How much money will you need for start-up?

- How much money will you need to stay in business until profits are realized?

Other questions that you will need to consider include:

- What are your sales and profit goals for the coming year?

- If a franchise, will the franchisor establish your sales and profit goals? Will they expect you to reach and retain a certain sales level and profit margin?

- What financial projections will you need to include in your business plan?

- What kind of inventory-control system will you use?

Your plan should include an explanation of all projections. Unless you are thoroughly familiar with financial statements, get help in preparing your cash flow and income statements as well as your balance sheet. Your aim is not to become a financial wizard, but to understand the financial tools well enough to gain their benefits. Your accountant or financial advisor can help you accomplish this goal.

Capital Equipment and Supply List

Capital equipment is any equipment with a useful life of one year or more that is used in the creation and sale of a product or service. Typically, "equipment" is freestanding and can be resold. For example, a glass display case is a capital equipment purchase, while an enlarged waiting room is a real property improvement.

If you aren't building new construction or undergoing an extensive building renovation, your biggest expenses will be furnishings and equipment. Start with a master wish list and your estimated costs for new and used equipment.

Think used. Unfortunately, the failure rate of businesses is significant enough that there is plenty of top-quality used equipment on the market at all times. Used equipment (especially for behind-the-scenes needs) is a wise investment.

Your supply list also includes the "consumables" that you'll need to set up an office, your kitchen, your factory, or your public areas. Consumables can be everything from toilet paper to printer ink cartridges (any non-saleable item that is used up and requires restocking). Such items as dinnerware, temporary décor, and promotional signs can be considered consumables as pieces become broken or worn.

CRUNCHING MORE NUMBERS

Many businesspeople look glassy-eyed when they sit down to create the financial reports needed to document their cash flow and income projections. Computer software makes it much easier.

For help with financial reporting and spreadsheet templates, check out:

- Intuit's QuickBooks Premier (**www.intuit.com**)

- PlanMagic Business Plan
  (**www.planmagic.com**)

- Virtual Business
  (**www.virtualbusiness.com/prices.htm**)

If accounting terms, ratios, and financial calculations aren't a normal part of your business vocabulary, purchase a basic accounting book such as *Understanding Business Accounting for Dummies*. You must know and understand these terms.

To prepare financial statements, you must make some basic assumptions upon from which to build. To estimate future sales, look at such factors as counts, turns, average order size, repeat visits, and ongoing automatic shipments.

Industry analysis, assumptions, and research are available from BizMiner at **www.bizminer.com**. Industry associations and the federal government also gather valuable data that you can use to create your plan. See Chapter 12 – *Business Plan References*.

INCOME PROJECTION

Your income projections serve as both a model for profitability and as a benchmark of your progress. If you have an existing business, you'll provide actual profit and loss statements along with income projections based upon historical data and upcoming activities, flavored with your vision of the future. Although new businesses won't have any history, you may have some data to use as a baseline if you are purchasing an existing business or investing in a franchise. Take what you do know and create some probable scenarios to project anticipated income and expenses for year one, year three, and year five.

Some projections will be based upon assumptions that are merely educated guesses. In this financial data section, you'll establish and define the important assumptions.

Your P&L projections will need to be created for the upcoming three years. For your first year of a new business, you'll need month-by-month statements. All businesses have sales cycles based upon the seasons, community events, and even the days of the week. Your month-by-month breakdown should take into account all anticipated external events that positively or negatively affect your sales. This first-year look is your benchmark period. You'll be able to compare your pro-forma projections with actual sales. This process will help you review and update your assumptions and projections.

The second and third years will need P&L statements by quarters, with a summary at the end of each year. The last income projection report will be a summary report that includes all three years.

Income Projection Statement

Income Statement — Summary for Years* Ending Dec 31						
	*9 Months Ended 2006	2007	2008	2009	2010	Totals
Sales Revenue						
Sales						
Total Sales						
Less Cost of Goods Sold						
Labor						
Supplies						
Total Cost of Goods Sold						
Gross Profit						
Operating Expenses						
Marketing and Promotion						
Insurance						
Telephone, Internet, Utilities						
Professional Fees						
Bank Charges						
Interest						
Depreciation						
Vehicle						
Repairs and Maintenance						
Other Wages						
CPP and Other Benefits						

Income Statement — Summary for Years* Ending Dec 31						
	*9 Months Ended 2006	2007	2008	2009	2010	Totals
Operating Expenses (continued)						
Membership and Professional Associations						
Bad Debt Expenses						
Miscellaneous						
Total Operating Expenses						
Income (Loss) Before Taxes						
Income Taxes						
Net Income (Loss)						
Cumulative Net Income (Loss)						

1. **Total Net Sales**

   Determine the total number of units of products or services you realistically expect to sell each month.

2. **Cost of Sales**

   Calculate cost of sales of all products and services used to determine total net sales. Include transportation costs and direct labor.

3. **Gross Profit**

   Subtract the total cost of sales from the total net sales.

4. **Gross Profit Margin**

   The gross profit is expressed as a percentage of total sales (revenues).

   gross profits / total net sales

5. **Variable and Fixed Expenses**

   Estimate your monthly expense and make sure to account for seasonal differences.

6. **Net Profit (loss) before taxes**

   Subtract total expenses from gross profit.

7. **Taxes**

   Include inventory and sales tax, excise tax, real estate tax, etc.

8. **Net Profit (loss) after taxes**

   Subtract taxes from net profit (before taxes).

Excerpt Alert

Income Statement — Summary for Years* Ending Dec 31						
	*9 Month Ended 2006	2007	2008	2009	2010	Totals
Sales Revenue						
Sales	27,000	48,000	60,000	75,000	93,750	303,750
Total Sales	27,000	48,000	60,000	75,000	93,750	303,750
Less Cost of Goods Sold						
Labor	12,420	22,080	27,600	34,500	43,125	139,725
Supplies	2,025	3,600	4,500	5,625	7,031	22,781
Total Cost of Goods Sold	14,445	25,680	32,100	40,125	50,156	162,506
Gross Profit						
	12,555	22,320	27,900	34,875	43,594	141,244
Operating Expenses						
Marketing and Promotion	1,620	2,880	3,600	4,500	5,625	18,225
Insurance	400	450	500	600	775	2,725
Telephone, Internet, Utilities	810	1,440	1,800	2,250	2,813	9,113
Professional Fees	540	960	1,200	1,500	1,875	6,075
Bank Charges	150	264	330	413	516	1,673
Interest	0	0	0	0	0	0
Depreciation	3,000	4,000	6,500	6,500	6,500	26,500
Vehicle	810	1,440	1,800	2,250	2,813	9,113
Repairs and Maintenance	810	1,440	1,800	2,250	2,813	9,113
Other Wages	0	0	0	0	0	0

Income Statement — Summary for Years* Ending Dec 31						
	*9 Month Ended 2006	2007	2008	2009	2010	Totals
Operating Expenses (continued)						
CPP and Other Benefits	225	492	687	945	1,207	3,556
Membership and Professional Associations	750	825	900	975	1,050	4,500
Bad Debt Expenses	270	480	600	750	937	3,037
Miscellaneous	540	960	1,200	1,500	1,875	6,075
Total Operating Expenses	9,925	15,631	20,917	24,433	28,799	99,705
Income (Loss) Before Taxes						
	2,630	6,689	6,983	10,443	14,795	41,539
Income Taxes	421	1,070	1,117	1,671	2,367	6,646
Net Income (Loss)						
	2,209	5,619	5,866	8,772	12,428	34,894
Cumulative Net Income (Loss)						
	2,209	7,828	13,694	22,466	34,894	34,894

BALANCE SHEET

A balance sheet is just that — a statement where all assets are listed and weighed against all liabilities. Assets minus liabilities equal net worth as of a specific date. Accounting software can create a balance sheet quickly and easily.

Balance Sheet Statement

Balance Sheet - As of _____						
ASSETS						
Current Assets						
Cash						
Accounts Receivable, Net						
Supplies Inventory						
Other						
Total Current Assets						
Long-Term Assets						
Vehicle						
Less Accumulated Depreciation						
Net Vehicle						
Equipment						
Less Accumulated Depreciation						
Net Equipment						
Other Long-Term Assets						
Total Long-Term Assets						
Total Assets						

Balance Sheet - As of _____						
LIABILITIES AND SHAREHOLDERS' EQUITY						
Current Liabilities						
Short-Term Debt						
Current Maturities of Long-Term Debt						
Accounts Payable						
Income Taxes Payable						
Other						
Total Current Liabilities						
Long-Term Liabilities						
Long-Term Debt less Current Maturities						
Other Long-Term Liabilities						
Total Long-Term Liabilities						
Owner's Equity						
Capital						
Retained Earnings						
Other						
Total Owner's Equity						
Total Liabilities and Shareholders' Equity						

ASSETS

List anything of value that is owned or legally owed to the business. Assets are listed at net value, so subtract depreciation and amortization from the original costs of acquiring the assets.

Current Assets

Cash — Money on hand and deposits in the bank.

Accounts receivable — The amounts due from customers in payment for merchandise or services.

Inventory — Includes raw materials on hand; work in progress; and all finished goods, either manufactured or purchased for resale.

Short-term investments — Holdings expected to be converted into cash within a year.

Prepaid expenses — Goods, benefits, or services a business buys or rents in advance. Examples are office supplies, insurance protection, and floor space.

Long-term assets — Holdings the business intends to keep for at least a year.

Fixed assets (also called **plant and equipment**) — Includes all resources a business owns or acquires for use in operations and not intended for resale.

Land — List original purchase price without allowances for market value.
- Buildings
- Improvements
- Equipment
- Furniture
- Automobile and vehicles

Liabilities

Current liabilities — List all debts, monetary obligations, and claims payable within 12 months.

Accounts payable — Amounts owed to suppliers for goods and services purchased in connection with business operations.

Notes payable — The balance of principal due to pay off short-term debt for borrowed funds.

Interest payable — Any accrued fees due for use of both short- and long-term borrowed capital as well as for any credit extended to the business.

Taxes payable — Amounts estimated by an accountant to have been incurred during the accounting period.

Payroll accrual — Salaries and wages currently owed.

Long-term liabilities — List notes, contract payment, or mortgage payments due over a period exceeding 12 months or one cycle of operation. They are listed by outstanding balance less the current position due.

Net Worth

Net worth (also called owner's equity) — Net worth is the claim of the owner(s) on the assets of the business. In a proprietorship or partnership, equity is each owner's original investment plus any earnings after withdrawals.

Total liabilities and net worth — The sum of these two amounts must always match that of total assets.

Excerpt Alert

Cash Flow Forecast - For the Years* Ending Dec 31						
	*9 Months Ended 2006	2007	2008	2009	2010	Totals
Receipts						
Cash Sales, Net Bad Debts	22,980	46,270	58,150	72,687	90,860	267,967
Owner Investment	1,000		0	0	0	1,000

Cash Flow Forecast - For the Years* Ending Dec 31						
	*9 Months Ended 2006	2007	2008	2009	2010	Totals
Receipts (continued)						
Loans Received	0	0	0	0	0	0
Other	0	0	0	0	0	0
Total Receipts	23,980	46,270	58,150	72,687	90,860	267,967
Payments						
Supplies	2,025	3,600	4,500	5,625	7,031	20,756
Direct Labor	12,420	22,080	27,600	34,500	43,125	127,305
Capital Purchases	0	5,000	5,000	0	0	10,000
Payments to Creditors	0	0	0	0	0	0
Loan Repayments	0	0	0	6,666	6,667	13,333
Marketing and Promotion	1,620	2,880	3,600	4,500	5,625	16,605
Insurance	400	450	500	600	775	2,325
Telephone, Internet, Utilities	810	1,440	1,800	2,250	2,813	8,303
Professional Fees	540	960	1,200	1,500	1,875	2,160
Bank Charges	150	264	330	413	516	1,523
Vehicle	810	1,440	1,800	2,250	2,813	8,303
Repairs and Maintenance	810	1,440	1,800	2,250	2,813	8,303

Cash Flow Forecast - For the Years* Ending Dec 31						
	*9 Months Ended 2006	2007	2008	2009	2010	Totals
Payments (continued)						
CPP and Other Benefits	225	492	687	945	1,207	3,331
Other Wages	0	0	0	0	0	0
Membership and Professional Associations	750	825	900	975	1,050	3,750
Miscellaneous	540	960	1,200	1,500	1,875	5,535
Tax payments	421	1,070	1,117	1,671	2,367	6,226
Owner's Drawings	0	0	0	0	0	0
Total Payments	21,521	42,901	52,034	65,645	80,552	237,758
Cash Flow Surplus/ Deficit (−)	2,459	3,369	6,116	7,042	10,308	26,834
Opening Cash Balance	0	2,459	5,828	11,944	18,986	39,217
Closing Cash Balance	2,459	5,828	11,944	18,986	29,294	57,761

PRO-FORMA CASH FLOW

Pro-forma refers to a financial document prepared in advance to use as a basis for decision-making or fiscal activities. Incoming cash flow is the money that comes in from sales, investors, loans, or sale of assets. Outgoing cash flow is the money that goes out in the payments and cash expenditures to pay suppliers, employees, long-term debts, and taxes.

Insufficient or inconsistent incoming cash can cripple a business. Understanding and monitoring your cash flow may actually be a better predictor of your financial success than a P&L statement. Although the business is profitable on paper, if the cash isn't available when bills are due, the business is in financial distress.

Net cash flow is the difference between incoming cash and outgoing cash. Start-up costs and unforeseen expenses during your launch can quickly gobble up your cash. Preparing cash flow reports will help you discover periods where working capital can keep your bills paid on time and paychecks funded.

Cash Flow Statement

Cash Flow Forecast – 12 Months			
Month:			
Sources of Cash:			
Cash Sales, Net Bad Debts			
Owner Investment			
Loans Received			
Other			
Total Receipts			
Uses of Cash:			
Supplies			
Direct Labor			
Capital Purchases			
Payments to Creditors			
Loan Repayments			
Marketing and Promotion			
Insurance			
Telephone, Internet, Utilities			
Professional Fees			
Bank Charges			
Vehicle			
Repairs and Maintenance			
CPP and Other Benefits			
Other Wages			
Membership and Professional Associations			
Miscellaneous			
Tax Payments			
Owner's Drawings			
TOTAL PAYMENTS			

Cash Flow Forecast – 12 Months			
(continued)			
Cash Flow Surplus/Deficit (-)			
Opening Cash Balance			
Closing Cash Balance			

Enter cash on hand (beginning of month)

Cash receipts

Cash sales — Omit credit sales unless cash is actually received.

Loan or other cash injection.

Calculate total cash receipts

Cash paid out

Purchases (merchandise) — Merchandise for resale or for use in product (paid for in current month).

Enter Operating Expenses paid (utilities, wages, etc.).

Enter Financing Expenses paid (loan payments, etc.).

Calculate total cash paid out

Excerpt Alert

Month:	Pre-Start	Apr-06	May-06	Jun-06	Jul-06	Aug-06	Feb-07	Mar-07
Cash Flow Forecast – 12 Months								
Sources of Cash:								
Cash Sales, Net Bad Debts		720	1,470	2,970	2,970	2,970	3,460	3,960
Owner Investment	1,000	0	0	0	0	0	0	0
Loans Received	0	0	0	0	0	0	0	0
Other	0	0	0	0	0	0	0	0
Total Receipts	1,000	720	1,470	2,970	2,970	2,970	3,460	3,960
Uses of Cash:								
Supplies	225	200	200	200	200	200	280	280
Direct Labor	0	0	0	1,620	1,800	1,800	1,840	1,840
Capital Purchases	0	0	0	0	0	0	0	0
Payments to Creditors	0	0	0	0	0	0	0	0
Loan Repayments	0	0	0	0	0	0	0	0
Marketing & Promotion	270	150	150	150	150	150	240	240
Insurance	400	0	0	0	0	0	0	0
Telephone, Internet, Utilities	0	90	90	90	90	90	120	120
Professional Fees	0	250	0	0	0	0	0	0

Cash Flow Forecast – 12 Months							
Month:	Pre-Start	Apr-06	May-06	Jun-06	Jul-06	Aug-06	Feb-07	Mar-07
Uses of Cash (continued)								
Bank Charges	60	10	10	10	10	10	6	6
Vehicle	0	90	90	90	90	90	120	120
Repairs and Maintenance	0	90	90	90	90	90	120	120
CPP and Other Benefits	0	0	0	0	0	0	0	0
Other Wages	0	0	0	0	0	0	0	0
Membership and Professional Associations	510	0	0	240	0	0	0	0
Misc.		60	60	60	60	60	80	80
Tax Payments	0	0	0	0	0	0	0	0
Owner's Drawings	0	0	0	0	0	0	0	0
Total Payments	1,465	940	690	2,550	2,490	2,490	2,806	2,806
Cash Flow Surplus/Deficit (–)	(465)	(220)	780	420	480	480	654	1,154
Opening Cash Balance	0	(465)	(685)	95	515	995	1,475	2,129
Closing Cash Balance	(465)	(685)	95	515	995	1,475	2,129	3,283

FINANCIAL ASSUMPTIONS

Your pro-forma statements are by definition based on certain assumptions. Be sure to include a list of your assumptions in your business plan. This way, readers can make sense of your numbers and know that they have some basis in fact.

Excerpt Alert

Revenue Assumptions

Year 1:	$3000.00/month	
Year 2:	$4000.00/month	33% anticipated business growth
Year 3:	$5000.00/month	25% anticipated business growth
Year 4:	$6250.00/month	25% anticipated business growth
Year 5:	$7812.50/month	25% anticipated business growth

Assumptions Regarding the Collection of Sales Revenue

a. We assume that the percentage of sales that are collected in the month they are made, in the month following, and in the three months are:

Current Month .25%

Following Month 25%

3rd Month 50%

This will create Accounts Receivable balances as follows:

Year 1 . . . .$3750

Year 2 . . . .$5000

Year 3 . . . .$6250

Year 4 . . . .$7813

Year 5 . . . .$9766

Cost of Sales and Expense Assumptions

These figures show up on the Income and Cash Flow Statements.

ITEM	PERCENT OF SALES OR OTHER
COST OF GOODS	
Labor	46%
Supplies	7.5%
Total Cost of Goods	54%
OPERATING EXPENSES	
Marketing and Promotion	6%
Insurance	Minimum coverage rate plus annual increases
Telephone, Internet, Utilities	3%
Professional Fees	2%
Bank Charges	0.55%
DEPRECIATION (See discussion next page)	
Vehicle	3%
Repairs and Maintenance	3%
Other Wages	0%

CPP AND OTHER BENEFITS

Assumed 7% increase per year of basic rate with $3,500 exemption per year.

MEMBERSHIP & ASSOCIATIONS

3 associations at a $25/year fee increase for each

Bad Debt 1%

Miscellaneous 2%

FIXED ASSETS, CAPITAL PURCHASES, AND DEPRECIATION ASSUMPTIONS

Depreciation is based on the Straight-Line method

ASSETS AT START-UP:

Vehicle . . . . 20% per year, 5-year life span

Equipment . . . . 20% per year, 5-year life span

CAPITAL PURCHASES:

$ 5,000—Laptop computer and software
　　　　　　Purchased with cash

20% depreciation per year, 5-year life span

$25,000—Vehicle
　　　　　Purchased with $5,000 cash down payment
　　　　　and 3-year interest-free loan from parents on
　　　　　$20,000 balance

10% depreciation per year, 10-year life span

FINANCIAL SOFTWARE HELP

You'll find financial templates on the enclosed CD along with the planning reports available on all business accounting packages. PlanWare at **www.planware.org** has a variety of software financial projection planners including various cash flow planning tools for United States, Canadian, and U.K. users.

MISTAKES TO AVOID

- **Not asking for what you want.** Be specific about the amount of money you are seeking.

- **Not detailing your spending.** Outline what you will use the money for and why you will spend it that way.

- **Not accounting for all start-up costs.**

- **Inadequate cash flow.** Your sales may be skyrocketing and profits way up, but if you don't have adequate cash flow (cash that comes in regularly to pay for recurring payables), your business can collapse.

- **Over-outfitting your operation.** Start by budgeting for your "must have" equipment. This may mean purchasing used equipment or waiting to purchase state-of-the-art versions. Don't over-invest in equipment and deplete your start-up capital.

- **Forgetting key financial reports.** Your **FAST PLAN** must include an income statement, balance sheet, and cash flow statement.

- **Failing to tell where the numbers come from.** Clearly explain the financial assumptions behind your projections. These may come from historical data (for active businesses) or your industry research (for new businesses).

- **Insufficient owner investment.** Financial participants will expect you to provide the lion's share of start-up capital.

- **Ignoring worst-case scenarios.** The business world is filled with ups and downs. Your plan needs to address both.

chapter 9

PUT IT ALL TOGETHER

***T**he research and writing are complete*; now it's time to put it all together in one cohesive package. To finish your business plan, you need to create:

- Cover page

- Table of contents

- Executive summary

- Conclusion

- Support documents

Cover Page

You'll need to include your legal business name, assumed business name (also known as "doing business as" or DBA), owner name(s), contact address, phone, fax, and e-mail information.

Table of Contents

The last page you will write for your plan.

EXECUTIVE SUMMARY

The Executive Summary is an abbreviated version of the entire plan, written to catch the attention of investors and lenders. Interested parties will read this mini-plan first (and often never go beyond it), so it is imperative that the Executive Summary be a strong distillation of your research and plans for success.

An Executive Summary ranges from a few paragraphs to a few pages. Often this recap section is written after the balance of the plan is completed.

In creating a 60-minute **FAST PLAN**, concentrate on writing at least a one-page Executive Summary. It must contain everything you'd want the reader to know quickly. Present factual information with a clear, confident tone and include some of your passion. Don't bog people down with dull facts here—give them the important highlights. Assume that the reader won't go any further than this page.

Executive Summary

The Opportunity

Advanced Business Solutions will establish itself as a provider of professional, high-quality management consulting and business services to organizations primarily within the Morrison, Pennsylvania, area. This business opportunity exists because:

Advanced Business Solutions can provide local access to high-quality management consultation and business services.

Advanced Business Solutions can provide these services at affordable rates due to low overhead and customized rate structures.

Advanced Business Solutions' owner has the breadth of experience and skills necessary to provide valuable assistance to community businesses and organizations.

Business Description

Advanced Business Solutions is a new business located in Morrison, Pennsylvania, providing customized management consultation and project facilitation to organizations within the city. Primary services will include Human Resource Management Outsourcing, Strategic Analysis and Planning, and Management Systems Analysis and Design.

Mission Statement: To provide professional management consulting and business services that enable clients to identify and capitalize on opportunities and achieve their operational goals.

Advanced Business Solutions will be located in the home of J. Jaxson, keeping the overhead low and the rates affordable. The home office has all the equipment necessary including a computer with professional Office Suite software, accounting software, design software, Internet and e-mail access, facsimile machine, laser and color-photo printers, and a photocopier.

Ownership and Management

Advanced Business Solutions is a sole proprietorship, owned by J. Jaxson. As the business expands, the firm may develop strategic alliances with other companies providing specialized services to businesses in Morrison. Jaxson has a master's degree in Business Administration (MBA), a bachelor's degree in Psychology, and is a member of the Beta Gamma Sigma honors society for business graduates.

J. Jaxson has consulted on a few projects within Morrison, managed the Human Resource function at the former NAYA water bottling facility, and taught and coordinated several business and computer courses at the local Okanagan University College campus. She has lived in Morrison for seven years and understands the issues facing local businesses. Advanced Business Solutions will initially have one employee, J. Jaxson. Additional staff support will be obtained on a subcontract basis as needed.

Marketing Opportunities

Morrison is not currently serviced by any professional management-consulting firms. Organizations seeking short-term, project-based management assistance need to contract out-of-town companies to provide these types of services. Morrison officers and business leaders are actively seeking business development and expansion opportunities, thus creating an opportunity for a small, local consulting firm such as Advanced Business Solutions. Few businesses in Morrison can afford to have professional managers on staff and will benefit from having access to this kind of expertise on a short-term or contract basis. Advanced Business Solutions will also be able to complete many of the necessary projects that tend to get put on hold due to lack of current resources: human or financial.

Competitive Advantages

The key competitive advantages of Advanced Business Solutions are the management experience, qualifications, and expertise of J. Jaxson; the business's relatively low overhead costs compared to large or out-of-town, competitive consulting firms; and the ability to provide customized business services.

J. Jaxson is a highly trained business professional with extensive relevant management experience. Overhead costs are comparatively low because Advanced Business Solutions will be based at the home of J. Jaxson, and because the firm is local, clients will not incur any additional travel or accommodation expenses. Customized business services will be available to help clients with many business projects, enabling operational goals to be met in an efficient, timely, and cost-effective manner.

Marketing Strategy

The target market will be established businesses or organizations within the Morrison area. Advanced Business Solutions will market its services by developing an introductory business flyer and distributing it through the local Chamber of Commerce, placing an ad in the local newspapers, networking with the local business community, and becoming an active member of a consulting association.

Advanced Business Solutions will expand on its introduction flyer by creating a detailed business package outlining the services and fee structure and highlighting the past experience and level of expertise of J. Jaxson. This package will be distributed to local business associations, lending institutions, key business leaders, and potential clients.

J. Jaxson will join local business associations to maintain contacts in the business community as well as to stay well informed about the business issues that are important to local businesses.

To attract more clients and increase revenue generation as necessary, Advanced Business Solutions will subscribe to online consulting and technical writing procurement services designed to bring service providers and clients together to complete projects using the Internet as the medium for exchange. Within the next two years, Advanced Business Solutions may develop an Internet site highlighting key services, level of expertise, and fee structure.

Summary of Financial Projections

The revenue of Advanced Business Solutions is projected to increase from $27,000 in the 9-month period ending December 31, 2006, to $93,750 by 2011.

Revenues will see strong growth of 25 percent (33 percent from 2006 to 2007) annually as the business grows and expands.

The Cost of Sales are 54 percent, including Direct Labor (including subcontractors) at 46 percent and Supplies at 7.5 percent.

The Net Income is projected to increase from $2,209 in 2006 to $12,428 in 2011. Corporate profits will be taxed at the corporate rate of 16 percent while J. Jaxson's wages of $40,000 per year will be taxed at prevailing personal tax rates.

Key Initiatives and Objectives

Advanced Business Solutions is currently operating with an initial owner's investment of $16,225 in office equipment, business vehicle, and cash. The key objective during the first 12 months of operation is to develop a profitable consulting business. To do this, a strong client base will be developed through networking with local business leaders and business associations, advertising in local newspapers, affiliating with small business loan divisions of the local banks, and joining Web-based contracting services as suitable.

Recognition of Risks

This business plan represents J. Jaxson's best estimate of the future of Advanced Business Solutions. It should be recognized that not all major risks can be predicted or avoided and few business plans are free of errors of omission or commission.

COMING TO A CONCLUSION

Your conclusion isn't just the end of your written business plan; it is a recap of the points you made that proves your plan to be viable and profitable. Your conclusion is also your opportunity to ask again for what you want and why you want it.

I am seeking a $50,000 capital improvement loan to complete the renovation of the historic Adams building. This represents 40 percent of the funds needed for this project and would provide Provencal with a new bar and increased customer capacity.

SUPPORT DOCUMENTS

This section includes various personal financial documents, legal documents, and other items that support your statements within the plan. Examples are listed below. You may have other documents that will give your lender or investor additional information of importance.

- Personal tax returns of the principals (owners) for the last three years.

- Business tax returns for the last three years (if you are already operational).

- Personal financial statements for each principal, detailing your assets and liabilities.

- Copy of franchise contracts and documents supplied by the franchisor (if applicable).

- Copy of proposed lease or purchase agreement for building space and/or land.

- Copy of licenses and other legal documents.

- Copy of résumés of all principals.

- Copy of résumés of key employees.

- Copies of letters of intent from suppliers, etc.

Note: Never attach originals unless they can be easily reproduced.

Writing a business plan is hard work, but the time and energy invested will result in a definitive return. The remaining chapters provide some additional tools to use when writing your plan. A comprehensive business plan will serve your business's needs for many years to come.

MISTAKES TO AVOID

- **Relying on unrelated successes.** A solid business background is invaluable, but don't rely too much on success in unrelated industries.

- **Not understanding how your industry works.** Basic industry knowledge is a must and should be demonstrated within the plan directly through the biographical sections and indirectly when you present your concept.

- **Arrogance.** A plan that implies that "not investing" would be a mistake is a big turn-off.

- **Too much name-dropping.** It takes more than a big-name customer or fan to become successful.

- **Unwilling to share ownership.** Investors (and some key management team members) will want a share of ownership.

- **Hiring unqualified family or friends.** Family and friends may be willing to work longer hours at lower pay to help you launch your business; however, unqualified key personnel are not a good financial risk for you or your investor or lender.

MISTAKES TO AVOID (continued)

- **No team.** Even independent contractors and one-person businesses need some outside support. Be certain to include attorneys, accountants, and consultants who can help you become successful.

- **Forgetting "Plan B."** When writing a *FAST PLAN*, you may be tempted to only talk about a rosy (and profitable) future. This is a mistake, because lenders and investors need to know that you can handle unforeseen situations or business obstacles.

- **Not addressing potential negatives.** Even the greatest inventions and ideas have some downsides. You will need to address these and offer solutions. This also demonstrates that you have the ability to learn and grow along with your business.

- **Looking too far into the future.** Discussing your company's future is important. However, if your historical performance or anticipated start-up success doesn't support your long-term projections, you'll be seen as naïve and unprofessional.

MISTAKES TO AVOID (continued)

- **No exit strategy.** It may seem odd to consider your plan for departure when writing a plan for a new business, but your exit strategy should deal briefly with what you would do if your business went public, or if you retired, or became unable to work. Investors need to know that the company has a future beyond your participation.

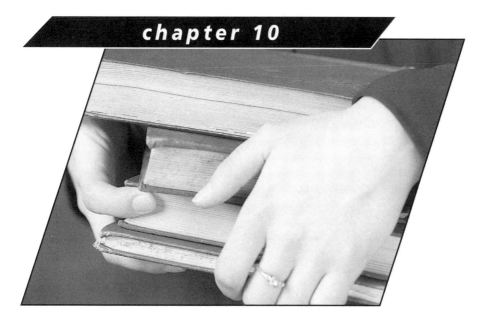

chapter 10

RESEARCHING YOUR PLAN

It may have been years since you wrote a term paper, but those creative data-gathering methods and research techniques will still prove useful. Your goal is to have all the information you need to "prove your thesis" when you sit down to write your **FAST PLAN**.

In writing a business plan, your "thesis" isn't a complex theoretical statement. Instead, it is a simple thought: "My idea for a [insert your concept here] business is a profitable one." Your research goal is to prove this statement accurate. If you cannot, then you need to rethink your idea and revise it.

In writing a **FAST PLAN**, the time you spend researching your business concept will take more than an hour — how much time you spend depends upon your current knowledge of the industry, the type of industry, and the resources available to you. However, you can keep yourself on track and save time by following the tips in this book.

Start researching via the Internet during your spare time. Using your favorite search engine, enter a variety of descriptive keywords or even type in questions. Bookmark and catalog your research for fast access when writing your plan. Review the resource list in Chapter 12 – *Business Plan References*.

If you choose to print out Web pages, reports, etc., use a highlighter pen on the key points of the document. File the printouts by subtopic so you can quickly scan each when the need arises.

GETTING ORGANIZED

Creating a data-gathering and filing system from the get-go will save time and make the writing process easier. To follow are some practical tips to get you started on creating a filing system that is comfortable to use and making using it a habit.

While you are actively exploring your business dream, you'll find that ideas pop into your head as you drive, just before you drop off to sleep, and at other unusual times. To record your ideas, consider purchasing a micro-recorder at a local office supply or electronic store.

Never leave home without:

- Notepad and pen (or micro-recorder) — All ideas have merit so don't censor yourself. Leave reminders here and follow up at the end of the day.

- Business cards — Make it easy for people to get back to you with requested information.

- Expandable file folder — Information comes in all sizes and shapes, so just drop it in to sort at the end of the day.

Set up a business plan file cabinet.

- This can be a drawer in an existing file cabinet or a self-contained version.

- Create hanging files and file folders. Divide information into categories.

- Your categories can follow a business plan outline or be of your own creation.

Empty your mind, pockets, and folder daily.

- By taking a few minutes to review, sort, and file data gathered each day, you'll also be able to make notes and comments that may be lost to you weeks from now.

Create a contact list.

- Whether this is a small address book or an electronic personal digital assistant, start gathering and carrying your contact list.

- Ask for business cards when you meet people.

- Make notes so you'll remember how and why this person can be helpful.

- Get e-mail addresses and Web sites.

- Cross-index referrals. For instance, if Norman Taylor refers you to Jennie Donaldson, make a note so you can "name drop." "Hello, my name is [name]. I'm doing research for a new business I am launching and Norman Taylor of Taylor Accounting referred me to you as someone who might be able help me."

Buy and send thank-you notes.

- Your local stationery or office supply store will have professional-looking thank-you notes. Send one when someone goes out of his or her way to provide assistance. This polite act is a great way to start a buzz within your community about your new business.

Create a master to-do/reminder/follow-up list.

- At the end of the day, transfer your notes and audio memos to a master list. Don't wait too long or you'll forget what your scribbling means!

- Not every question can be answered in one phone call or visit, so a follow-up list will keep you from forgetting something.

- Research tends to lead to other research possibilities. Add these to your master to-do list.

Create a "Business Plan" favorites (bookmark) folder and e-mail inbox.

- An enormous amount of research information is available on the Internet. Create subtopic folders so you can categorize and find bookmarked sites quickly.

- A great organizational tool for Internet research is Onfolio at **www.onfolio.com**. You can flag sites by importance, write reminder descriptions, search your notes by keyword, and even save text from a site and file it.

If you are sending e-mails requesting information, sort your outgoing messages and incoming responses into a "Business Plan" inbox folder. Check your e-mail client software for ways to make this automatic.

CREATE A RESEARCH LIST

Your research list consists of questions that you don't know the answers to right now. The answers should prove:

- There is a need for your business.

- There are ample paying customers available to you.

- You can be competitive in pricing, service, and quality.

- Your location works for you and your future customers.

- You can make it happen.

Write down all the questions that your partners, lawyer, lender, investors, accountant, management team, creative personnel, and family might ask about your new or expanding business. Be prepared to answer them from memory.

To get you started, here are some typical questions to which you'll need answers:

- Is your desired location zoned for commercial activities?

- Will people want you to be open before or after work? weekends?

- Do you need to build your own facility, or can you find appropriate space to lease?

- Are your offerings too trendy? too late in the trend cycle?

- Will you have enough potential patrons who enjoy your products?

- How much will you have to spend to outfit your kitchen, storefront, office, or manufacturing plant?

- Will you need to register your name as a trademark or service mark?

- Will you be able to obtain a liquor license, zoning permit, or building permit?

- Are there environmental rules or other laws that will prohibit you from using a piece of equipment, creating waste, or hanging a sign?

- Can your products or service be competitively priced and profitable?

Assumptions Are Not Conclusions

When deciding what data you need to construct your business plan, don't make unnecessary assumptions. Assumptions, by definition, are personal beliefs not supported by fact. *Assuming that* you'll be able to get a needed code variance or your town needs another pizza parlor can be costly errors in judgment.

Assumptions aren't a reliable foundation for decision making and business success. If you believe something to be true, prove it! Unsupported claims may make your plan look strong, but they do everyone a disservice.

After researching your new business plan, you will be drawing some conclusions. Of course, these conclusions aren't going to be 100 percent accurate; however, if they are fact-based and reasonable, they will be what convinces your banker to lend you money and an investor to write you a check.

Ask for Help

Sometimes finding an answer can be difficult. However, a powerful research tool is readily available to you at no cost—asking for help. Ask politely and give people ample time to respond. You will be surprised at what you can learn. The help you receive can also come in the form of opinions, recommendations, and referrals to other resources.

Ask:

- **Family and friends.** Their opinions (even biased ones) may lead in you a specific direction.

- **Peers.** Their recommendations can save you time and money.

- **Trade and business organizations.** The National Business Association, local and national chambers of commerce, local and national Better Business Bureaus, and SCORE are just a few organizations designed to support small business. You will find a list of resources in Chapter 12.

- **Government agencies.** City, county, state, and national governmental bodies are the largest gatherers of information, and all of it is free. Finding the person who holds the key to the data can be worth the time spent standing in line or waiting on hold. Don't forget the Internet, as information and records are now transferred to online databases.

- **Educational sources.** Colleges and universities along with nonprofit foundations aimed at supporting small business endeavors can be very helpful.

- **Customers.** Take a survey of passersby or ask current customers their opinions.

- **Competitors.** Not all competitors are wary of your inquiries, but remember that it is rude to ask about confidential information.

A nice chat with a salesclerk or technician may give you the answer you need. Other information may be a matter of public record. Check with the appropriate government agency. Check private organizations such as Dun & Bradstreet (**www.smallbusiness.dnb.com**) and Hoovers Online (**www.hoovers.com**) for background information. Publicly held companies (including chain operations and franchises) are required to file financial reports for investors. You'll find a wealth of information on these entities online, including business "gossip."

- **Local businesses.** Locate a networking group of local businesses or other entrepreneur clubs.

Hiring Research Help

If the only free time you have to research your plan is after normal business hours, you'll be depending primarily upon Internet resources. Another option is to hire someone to assist you with your research. A professional researcher will have many resources from which to draw. To locate a local researcher, use a search engine with the keyword "researcher" and your city name or contact your local library or college for a referral. University business departments may be able to connect you with a graduate student interested in handling your research needs. Professional market research firms such as Market Research (**www.marketresearch.com**) or BizVida (**www.bizvida.com**) can assist with a wide variety of research topics.

Hire a Financial Expert

Working with a certified public accountant (CPA) is probably worth every cent. Even the most seasoned businessperson can benefit from hands-on number crunching and advice when it comes to financial projections that span five years or more. The most important aspect is to understand them and be able to analyze each easily.

If you are a new entrepreneur, make a wise investment in a couple of hours of one-on-one time with your CPA to learn accounting terms, how to read and interpret standard business reports (P&L, balance sheet, and various accounting formulas and ratios), and to develop intermediate financial decision-making skills.

If you want to go it alone, think about taking a business owners' class (locally or online) on understanding financial statements. Your local library or bookstore will also have such books as *Accounting for Dummies* by John A. Tracy and *Financial Statements for Non-Financial People: A Quick-and-Easy Guide to Reading a Financial Statement* by Ron Price.

chapter 11

WRITING TIPS

This chapter covers tips to help you get your thoughts onto paper along with information on writing a more comprehensive plan should the need arise.

Gather Your Data

If you haven't followed the research organization tips in Chapter 10, a good place to start is to sort your research and support materials into basic categories that coordinate with a standard business plan format (see Chapter 2). Information may be used in more than one section, but file it into the most logical category. Create a file folder or pocket folder for each category.

Next, go through each folder and organize your data based upon its potential value to your writing. Highlight important information and attach your notes and reminders to the related research materials. This will help you find what you need, when you need it.

Now is the time to create a list of any information that appears to be missing. You'll have this list to refer to when you revisit bookmarked Web sites, reread articles, and sort through notes during the writing process.

Blank Screen, Go Away

Writing doesn't come easily for many people. The blank piece of paper or computer monitor doesn't help. Here are a few tips:

- **Start with the easiest parts first.** Work on sections in any order you like.

- **Try writing in longhand.** The act of changing to a different medium can sometimes help. Not everyone feels comfortable at the keyboard. You may even want to write the entire document by hand and have a typist or consultant format everything for publication.

- **Write in a natural voice.** Although the language of business can be stiff and formal, don't let this become an obstacle. You can always go back and make it "sound professional" after you express your ideas and provide convincing arguments. Again, a business plan writer/consultant can take this and fashion a formal business plan.

- **Write what pops into your head.** Don't over-think: the first idea is often the best one. Get it written down and then think about how it can be improved.

Coping with Writers' Anxiety

Sometimes writers' block (where you cannot seem to get words on paper) turns into writers' anxiety. Purdue University offers some great tips on coping with the natural anxiety people feel when writing a boring yet important paper at **http://owl.english.purdue.edu/handouts/general/gl_anxiety.html**.

Writing Formally

- **Remove all the extra words.** A common mistake in business writing in a more formal tone is to add unnecessary words. See, I just didn't need those descriptive words to tell you what I meant. If in doubt, leave it out, and read the sentence aloud. If the thought is clear, you don't need it.

- **Set your spelling/grammar-checker to formal.** Some spell-checkers allow you to set the document style for word usage and grammar to formal styles where, for example, contractions are not (aren't) used.

Using an Outline Format

Automated outline formats are standard in word processing programs. The user manual or interactive help system can guide you on how to use this formatting tool.

THE MOST IMPORTANT ADVICE

- **Don't carry around all your notes, statistics, and research.** Even if you have time during a lunch break to work on your plan, your research and notes could be easily damaged or lost. If you must work away from your office or home, take copies of critical information and keep the originals intact.

- **Back up your work!** Take advantage of automated backup programs, online backup services, and even the basic floppy disk. Be certain to back up after each work session all accounting, spreadsheets, and written documents.

PUBLISH YOUR PLAN

Your business plan needs to be published. How you present your research, analysis, and business ideas play an important part in impressing lenders, investors, and others. A professional presentation tells people you are serious.

If you've used a word processor and written each section in a different file, combine the files in the proper order to create a master file. Once you have created a master business plan document, follow each step below in the order listed:

1. **Spell-check the entire document.** Using your word processor's built-in spelling, syntax, and grammar-checker will help you catch some (but never all) common mistakes. *Never rely on their accuracy.* Not only do they have problems with words that sound alike, but they also often get confused with more complex sentence structures. A dictionary, a thesaurus, and a grammar book should be your guides. Consider hiring a professional to edit your document.

2. **Read the entire document aloud.** This will help you "hear" areas that might confuse your target reader and catch grammatical errors. Proofing and reviewing your own writing can be difficult. Because you know what the plan is supposed to say, it is easy

for your mind to not "see" what is actually written. Have your spouse or a friend read for you so you can concentrate on listening to every word. Remember that your document will have a more formal tone than your normal speaking style.

3. **Review facts and figures.** Now is the time to double-check facts and figures, especially in the financial section.

4. **Check the layout.** The use of predefined styles can also make the process easier. However, layouts can wander off track during the entire process. To make your plan more visually appealing and professional looking:

   a. Verify your margin settings. You should have a two-inch left-hand margin to have ample room to punch or bind. Adjust your margin settings before you make any other layout changes.

   b. Go through each page and verify the Roman numerals assigned to each section and subsection.

   c. Look for "orphans and widows" in your layout. An orphan is single word on the last line at the bottom of a page. A widow is a single word or short phrase at the top of a page. Most word processors can be set to avoid orphans and widows.

d. **Check for consistency in titles, subtitles, and footnotes.** Most documents will be written in the standard business font, Times New Roman. You may have chosen another complementary font for titles. If you make your section titles Arial Bold and your subsection titles Arial Italics, they should follow the same convention. If titles are to be in all caps, check to see that each follows this standard.

5. **Create a table of contents.** Your table of contents will list each major section. You may also list select subsections if your plan is longer than ten pages. Microsoft Word has a table of contents feature, but you may find it easier to print the full report and write your own. Verify your page numbering accuracy for inserts created separately.

6. **Inserting cross-reference information.** If you refer to a section, subsection, or specific support document, you may want to insert the final page number along with the originating reference. Since you've verified the page numbering system, you'll now be able to direct the reader to the correct page.

formats can be used with their equipment.

Some copy centers will only print on paper purchased on site. If you want your report printed on letterhead, call the copy store first to negotiate this.

Paper, Please

Select a high-quality bond paper suitable for your chosen printer. Office supply stores have hundreds of options. The minimum quality level you should use (this also applies when selecting paper at the copy store) is white, 24-pound paper, which is heavier and more opaque than ordinary printer or copier paper. In addition, the paper you choose should have a brightness rating of 90 or higher. Select laser paper for laser output and inkjet paper for inkjet output.

Consider the stationery paper section at an office supply store This paper is more costly than the high-end printer paper described above, but it will add richness to your presentation.

Select either 24-pound white or ivory linen. Linen refers to the visible grain used in more expensive letterhead. Mass-market stationery paper will also list whether it is laser or inkjet compatible. If in doubt, purchase the minimum quantity and test it. Linen and other quality papers have more absorbent fibers, so your printer ink may bleed slightly, giving your document a hazy appearance.

Holding It All Together

Before you head to the presentation folder aisle, print a mock-up of your plan on your chosen paper. Then measure the plan's thickness with any support documents you need to include. If your plan is three-quarters of an inch thick, a one-inch binder will be ample. If in doubt, select the next larger size.

If you haven't put together a bound presentation in awhile, you'll be amazed at the options. There are ring binders, folders with windows, leather binders, folders with pockets, and more. (No sheet protectors, please.) The three-ring format is standardized so that any three-hole punch will work. Look for a suitable binder or folder that looks expensive but isn't. Colors such as black, dark brown, medium or dark blue, and maroon are all acceptable.

If you have bulky support documents unsuitable for hole-punching, there are presentation folders that have pockets. Remember not to include anything that you need returned.

If you'll be mailing or shipping your plan, pick up an appropriate padded envelope or shipping box.

Assembling Your Plan

You have printed your plan on elegant linen paper, purchased a professional-looking dark gray folder, and had full-color charts printed. Now assemble everything with the table of contents after your cover page. If your plan is more than an inch thick, include section dividers with labeled tabs. These are available at your office supply store in a variety of formats including those that will go through your laser printer. Make certain that you purchase the correct format and size for your ring binder and inserts.

BUSINESS PLAN = STRATEGIC PLAN

Your trimmed-down version of a traditional business plan can also be a powerful tool for making decisions and setting goals. A *FAST PLAN* can be written for:

- An introduction to your new business venture. Suitable for preliminary discussions with bankers, potential partners, and employee searches.

- A specific marketing campaign. To open a dialogue with an ad agency, marketing consultant, and business managers.

- A profit-enhancing plan. Use this to illustrate to employees how specific actions and changes can increase profits, which increase their salaries and bonuses.

- A business goal-setting plan. Share this with employees at every level to collect ideas, build consensus, explain rewards, and establish expectations.

- A personal goal-setting plan. Explore your personal goals and expectations. Should you delegate more to your employees and work less? Should you prepare to retire?

Half of the purpose of any plan is to force you to take time to think about the reasons for the plan. Clear your mind and concentrate to improve your decision-making abilities.

When you write your **FAST PLAN**, keep your audience in mind. Don't bore them with any unnecessary details. Whet their appetite, stimulate creativity, and sell them!

INTERNAL BUSINESS PLANS

An internal business plan is written as an in-house decision-making tool and feasibility study. Such questions as "Will increasing your dining room size pay for the renovations required? How long would it earn back the cost of a $5,000 piece of equipment? Should I spend more money on radio spots or local cable TV spots?" are addressed by an internal business plan.

Below are some resources to help you create an internal plan that will excite your team, improve your decision making, and increase your chances for success.

- A Business Leader's Dream Tool — **www.leadership-tools.com/business-plan-template.html**

- Miller Consulting's Internal Business Plan Manual — **www.internalbusinessplans.co.uk/manual.htm**

- Sales & Marketing Strategies — **www.sms-direct.com/business-plan-development3.htm**

- BusinessCase.com — **www.businesscase.com/html/irr.html**

- PlanWare — **www.planware.org/strategy.htm**

- BusinessBalls.com — **www.businessballs.com/freebusiness plansandmarketingtemplates.htm**

REVISING AND UPDATING YOUR BUSINESS PLAN

Plan B

You've just spent hours writing and rewriting your feasibility analysis (Chapter 5—*Market Analysis Summary*) only to realize that the numbers just aren't there. Common scenarios are that you won't have enough capital to keep afloat until you become profitable, or that the building you have selected won't accommodate enough people for the sales volume you need.

You are probably overwhelmed. However, you still have opportunity to perfect your business model and increase your chance for long-term success. Businesspeople who don't take planning seriously often stumble through this process with costly results.

What do you do? Create Plan B, of course! Plan B entails reviewing where you can make changes. Examine where your plan falls short. Do you need to rethink the renovation of a historic building? Do you need to delay your launch until you have an additional six months of working capital? Do you need to rein in your dreams and start with a more manageable plan? Your research may reveal ways that you hadn't even considered.

Lack of money can be a big obstacle, but it is not

you astray? Looking at what brought you to where you are and comparing it to your launch plan will help you make adjustments to bring you back on track or to lead you to bigger and better things.

Your first business plan included your financial projections for the first three years of operation. Compare this to your actual performance figures. You'll also be able to update figures based upon information you didn't have before.

Review the plan every six months during the first two or three years of operation. During the critical first three years, you may find it helpful to use the plan during quarterly accounting reviews. By keeping your plan fresh, you'll be able to keep your original mission in mind. Other benefits to keeping your business plan up to date are that you will be prepared for growth, for additional investment opportunities, or for selling your business should the need arise.

At the end of three years, plans often need major overhauls to be relevant to current business trends, the economy, and competitive factors. Look at your plan as a guide to healthy growth. Revisit some of your assumptions. Are they still valid? Reviewing how your business was positioned over the past three years and setting new goals for the next three to five years will help you stay profitable.

Some areas to revisit include:

- Have the neighborhood demographics changed?

- Have buying habits changed?

- Have current trends made your products or services obsolete?

- Have traffic flow patterns changed your customer averages?

- Would remodeling your business bring in new customers?

- Has your advertising brought in a sufficient number of new customers?

- Have you built a strong repeat business?

- Are competitors outperforming you?

- Have you outgrown your business facility?

- Should you hire additional staff and work less personally?

SHOULD YOU REWRITE YOUR PLAN?

Businesspeople who have embraced the power of a written plan typically revise and even totally rewrite their plan when its contents have become dated and irrelevant. This may be in a year or five years — only you can determine the value for yourself.

Rewriting your plan offers the same benefits as when you created the original one:

- **Clarity.** A clear view of your goals and the paths to reach them.

- **Concentration.** Time set aside specifically for review, reflection, and projection.

- **Confidence.** Establishes what you do best and focuses on those skills and talents.

- **Commitment.** Rededicating yourself, your resources, and your team to a shared success.

chapter 12

BUSINESS PLAN
REFERENCES

Technically, all you need is a word processor, a calculator, and a printer to produce a professional-looking business plan. With this book, your personal records, and a few online reference sites, you will be able to write your own business plan from scratch.

FAST PLAN COMPANION CD

The companion CD contains a sample business plan in Word and financial spreadsheets in Excel to help you create a **FAST PLAN** business plan.

1. Cover sheet

2. Statement of purpose

3. Table of contents

4. Business information

   a. Description of business

   b. Operating procedures

   c. Personnel

   d. Marketing

   e. Competition

   f. Business insurance

5. Financial Data

   a. Loan applications

   b. Capital equipment and supply list

   c. Balance sheet

   d. Break-even analysis

   e. Pro-forma income projections (profit and loss statements)

      i. Three-year summary

      ii. Detail by month, first year

      iii. Detail by quarters, second and third years

      iv. Assumptions upon which projections were based

   f. Pro-forma cash flow

6. Supporting documents

   a. Tax returns of principals for past three years

   b. Personal financial statement

   c. For franchise businesses, a copy of franchise contract

   d. Franchisor-supplied documents

   e. Copy of proposed lease or purchase agreement for building space

   f. Copy of licenses and other legal documents

   g. Copy of résumés of all principals

   h. Copy of letters of intent from suppliers, etc.

ADDITIONAL BUSINESS PLAN RESOURCES

Accounting

- E-Z Projection — financial analysis software — **www.summitpublishing.com**

Advertising

- *How to Use the Internet to Advertise, Promote and Market Your Business or Web Site–With*

Little or No Money. Available from Atlantic Publishing for $24.95 (Item # HIA-01). To order call 1-800-814-1132 or visit www .atlantic-pub.com.

- Business Marketing — **www.businessmarketing.com**

- *Business Marketing for Owners and Managers* (Wiley Business Basics Series) by Patti J. Shock, John T. Bowen, John M. Stefanelli.

- *Your Business Marketing Genius at Work* — downloadable report — **www.Business Owner.com/downloads/special_report.pdf**

Books, Magazines, and Software

- Bplans.com — reseller for Palo Alto Software — **www.bplans.com**

- *Restaurant Operators Guide to QuickBooks* — **www.rrgconsulting.com**

- Megadox legal forms — **www.megadox.com/documents.php/97**

- Bulletproof Business Plans — **www.bulletproofbizplans.com**

Business Structure

- *Incorporating Your Business for Dummies* by

The Company Corporation (For Dummies Publisher)

- *AllBusiness.com Practical Guide to Incorporation* — **www.allbusiness.com/ guides/Incorporation.asp**

- Legal Spring consumer-oriented advice — **www.legalspring.com**

- Business Filings Incorporated — **www.bizfilings.com**

- My Corporation — **www.mycorporation.com**

- Corporate Creations — **www.corpcreations. com**

Feasibility Study Resources

- *Should I Start a New Business* — **www.mapnp.org/library/strt_org/prep.htm**

- *What Business Should I Start?* from The Planning Shop — **www.planningshop.com**

Financial Planning for Businesses

- Virtual Business — spreadsheets, advice, and planning tools — **www.virtualbusiness.com**

Government Resources

- Small Business Association (SBA) —

www.sba.gov

- Internal Revenue Service (IRS) — **www.irs.gov**

Industry Demographics and Research

- Biz Miner — **www.bizminer.com**

- National Business Association — **www.business.org/research**

- SBA — **www.sba.gov/starting_business/ marketing/research.html**

Research Methods

- Web Surveyor — **www.websurveyor.com**

Business Owner Support

- Business Owner — **www.businessowner.com**

- Business News — **www.businessnews.com**

- Idea Cafe — **www.businessownersideacafe.com**

- BizJournals — **www.bizjournals.com**

- Better Business Bureau — **www.bbbonline.org**

- Biz Talk — **www.biztalk.com**

- U.S. Chamber of Commerce — **www.uschamber.com**

- Entrepreneur — **www.entrepreneur.com**

- Rhonda Abrams (author and business columnist) — **www.rhondaonline.com**

- *Wall Street Journal* entrepreneur support — **http://startup.wsj.com**

- The Profit Center — **www.profitclinic.com**

- B2B Network for business professionals — **www.b2business.net**

Small Business Development and Support

- SCORE — **www.score.org**

- National Business Incubation Association — **www.nbia.org**

- Association for Enterprise Opportunity — support for small (five or fewer employers) businesses with start-up costs of $35,000 or less — **www.microenterpriseworks.org**

- Entrepreneur — offers general business and business specific guidance — **www .entrepreneur.com**

Business Plan Newsletters

- Free business plan newsletters **www .bizplanit .com/free/newsletter_request.html**

Business Plan Software

- BP-4-U — **www.businessplanning-4-you.com**

- *Business Plan Pro* (Palo Alto Software, **www.paloalto.com**)

- *Business Plan Writer Deluxe* (Nova Development, **www.novadevelopment.com**)

- *Ultimate Business Planner* (Atlas Business Solutions, Inc., **www.bptools.com**)

- *Plan Write* (Business Resource Software, **www.brs-inc.com**)

- *PlanMagic Business* (PlanMagic, **www. planmagic.com**) Word and Excel templates

Training Classes, Seminars, Workshops, and Web-Based Education

- NxLevel — free or low-cost business plan writing and entrepreneurial supporttraining — **www.nxlevel.org**

- FastTrack — Spanish and English programs and information — **www.fasttrac.org**

chapter 13

DOWN BY THE RIVER GIFT SHOP

"Take a Little of the River Home"

THIS BUSINESS PLAN CONTAINS
PROPRIETARY AND CONFIDENTIAL
INFORMATION BELONGING EXCLUSIVELY TO
"DOWN BY THE RIVER"

Proprietor: Sophie Vanden

Phone 217-555-5849
217-555-2436

Table of Contents

EXECUTIVE SUMMARY

This business proposal describes the plans for opening a retail establishment called "Down by the River," which will be located at 1111 River Road in Lynnville, Illinois. The objective of this proposal is to request a $55,000 working line of credit.

Down by the River will find its home on the banks of the Mississippi River, on historic River Road. Nested between several other quaint gift shops and eateries, Down by the River will offer original, one-of-a-kind, eclectic-river related gifts at affordable prices. A large selection of local artistry will be consigned as well as antiques. The inventory will reflect the local charm of river life and include a statuary of bald eagles and herons, sand art, and whimsical clothing.

The gift shop will be located in the historic Lynnville Granary Building, which is over 100 years old. Once a vital piece of Lynnville commerce directly on the riverfront, the interior has been completely renovated to accommodate a retail establishment. Restoration included salvaging the plank floors, hardware, and grain chutes. A large picture window and balcony were added for a spectacular view of the Mississippi River. Boat docks were recently added for boaters to come ashore. Boaters can walk right into the building to reach River Road.

Down by the River will be located at 1111 River Road in Lynnville, Illinois. The Lynnville Granary will be leased from the Julius family, which has owned the Granary since its construction. Lynnville is located within an hour of several large communities and is a common stop for an easy day trip. Winter and spring eagle watchers, bustling summer traffic from the river and street, and fall leaf-lookers make for a consistent customer base almost year-round.

The owner, Sophie Vanden, worked in various retail establishments for several years and has long had the ambition to open a gift shop on the banks of the Mississippi. When the Granary building came available, she knew this was her opportunity. Sophie plans to hire an assistant, Becca Timpton, who shares her ambition for a unique river-front store, and also plans to add two part-time employees.

Advertising will be done in three regional weekly newspapers, as well as several tourist guides for local Mississippi River towns. Promotions will focus on the short drive to Lynnville and the opportunity to "Take a Little of the River Home." Cooperative advertising with other local retailers promoting the town of Lynnville will also be explored.

STATEMENT OF PURPOSE

This Business Plan is being prepared to secure a $55,000 working line of credit.

Description of the Business

Down by the River features gifts that reflect the charm of living life on the river. Statuary, for inside and outside the home, of bald eagles, blue herons and egrets will be a large part of the inventory. Sand art (sand that has been formed into turtles, birds, and the like), as well as fishing items, are also featured. Antiques, especially fishing lures, poles and traps, and other river artifacts will be scattered throughout the store. In support of the local community, Down by the River will also feature consigned art, paintings, photographs, and more from local artists.

The functional side of Down by the River will include a small selection of fun and eclectic "river clothes." Unique and fun beach cover-ups, floppy sun hats, sunglasses, and sandals will be available for those who underestimate the power of sun and sand. Upscale, wearable souvenirs, like one-of-a-kind handcrafted jewelry will entice the fashionable.

Down by the River, which boasts "Take a Little of the River Home," truly has something for everyone — and at great prices.

Down by the River will be open 10 a.m. to 5 p.m., Monday through Friday; and 10 a.m. to 4 p.m. Saturday and Sunday, through the three peak seasons. Winter hours will be noon to 4 p.m., Thursday through Sunday.

Personal History

Sophie Vanden graduated from Illinois State University with a B.A. in Marketing in 1982. Her experience in marketing began at CTM, INC. (Consulting, Training and Marketing), a consulting firm that assists small businesses grow and increase their sales through seminars in training, advertising, and marketing. Sophie started in an entry-level position and was named Vice President before leaving in 1993 to meet the demands of her growing family. Sophie continued to teach seminars after taking her leave until the birth of her third child.

When her children were all in school, Sophie began working part time in various local retail stores. This gave her the opportunity to see firsthand what was missing on the River Front, and better yet, what was selling. She dreamed about the type of store that could be successful and secretly planned her staff and store.

When the Granary Building became available for lease, Sophie could not pass up the opportunity to turn her dream to reality in this prime retail location.

Business Name

The legal name of the business is "Down by the River."

Business Location

Sophie Vanden has leased the Lynnville Granary at 1111 River Road in Lynnville, Illinois, where "Down by the River" will be located.

Legal Form of Business

The legal form of business is a Sole Proprietorship, as registered in the state of Illinois.

Current Situation

With her experience in the marketing and retail industry, and a well-developed business plan, Sophie is well positioned to start a new business that will flourish. As the marketing analysis will show, Down by the River will fill a unique niche in a growing market. With her concept of "Take a Little of the River Home" and personal goals of something for everyone, Down by the River is sure to outshine her competitors. Sophie's marketing skills, as well as her hands-on learning of retail, will be the keys to her success.

The location in the Lynnville Granary will benefit from seasonal retail traffic as well as the local community. Replacing a previously held retail space will generate "accidental" repeat customers (those who were looking for the previous store). The boat docks on the river and the well-traveled River Road will also be a boon to clientele.

The Future/Goals

Sophie will not start small—her retail theory is "if it's full, you look like you are serious." Instead of a one-time customer, Sophie plans to cultivate a clientele of people who visit often, shop often, and buy often. By changing her inventory each season, and striving for something different every time, Sophie plans to generate excitement in her clients. Excitement that keeps them curious and anxious to come back, and excitement that they will share with friends and family.

INDUSTRY OVERVIEW

The Small Business Administration shows that 2004 was a year of transition, as signs of economic recovery began to appear in mid year. The number of firms grew, and business bankruptcies declined. Corporate profits were up, and sole proprietorship income increased by 6.2 percent. Trends in employment over the 2003–2004 period indicated that small firms fared better in some industries than in others. A look at this and other research on small businesses over the business cycle can help shed some light on small business directions for 2005 and beyond.

The financial markets were on track for supporting more growth in 2004, as low interest rates spawned corporate bond issues and generated a wave of mortgage refinancings by households. Equity markets began to rally, although this did not immediately translate into a stronger equity market for small firms. Lending to small businesses by banks showed little growth over the June 2003 to June 2004 period of observation (based on data availability), but this was expected, given that the economic pickup occurred later in the year.

Creating a Competitive Advantage

In an established, successful tourist town like Lynnville, Down by the River fills a niche with unique offerings. Customers who are looking for something different will find it—and they will find helpful, pleasant people to help them make purchases. A cup of coffee or lemonade adds to the homey atmosphere you rarely find elsewhere.

However, with an already-established retail community in Lynnville, other shops along River Road must compete or coexist. By finding the perfect mix of merchandise, one that is unique among the current retailers on River Road, Down by the River can happily coexist with other retailers. Having outstanding ambiance with the historic Granary, exclusive river access, and the perfect mix of merchandise, Down by the River will be the competition.

Outlook for Retail Establishments

Two-thirds of new small businesses survive at least two years, and about half survive at least four years. Owners of about one-third of retailers that closed said their business was successful at closure. Major factors contributing to a retailer remaining open include an ample supply of capital, the fact that it is large enough to have employees, the owner's education level, and the owner's reason for starting the firm in the first place, such as freedom for family life or wanting to be one's own boss.

Keeping Up with Customers

Customers' desire for uncommon items and one-on-one personal assistance drives the growth of small businesses across the nation. As the number of people employed outside the home increases, so does the need for convenience. Running in to the local store that has just what they need is far more convenient than driving farther and wading through department stores that have everything, but often not exactly what they are looking for.

For this reason, small businesses that offer a large selection and competitive pricing are widely successful. Small businesses are often known for the knowledgeable salespeople in the store who can offer advice and instruction to their customers. Strong customer service is key in a business where the owner often has a personal stake in the business's success.

Changing Customer Needs

As with any market analysis, the ability to focus on consumers' preferences is critical, particularly if customers tend to be repeat customers. In a 2004 Small Business Association survey, more than 87 percent of retailers reported introducing new lines of merchandise, and 74 percent plan to do so in the future.

Convenience and competitiveness are probably the most important features of a successful business. Retailers cannot afford to ignore the importance of pricing and the consumer's perception of the value for the dollar.

Finding and Keeping Good Help

The labor pool for retailers has remained competitive. In most regions and settings, entry-level jobs are considered temporary work for the youth labor pool. The second source for retailers is a small segment of homemakers and retirees that reside in the area.

After recruiting and training help, it is essential to

retain the new employees. Developing employee/ employer relations is important in gaining loyalty. Strong training in customer service and employee perks is essential to maintaining a high-quality staff that offers high-quality service.

Competition

A survey of the competition clearly indicates that Down by the River will fill a unique niche in the Lynnville community. No gift shop in Lynnville offers such a wide array of merchandise with such competitive pricing. By offering river antiques and exclusive consignments from local artisans, Down by the River will have the corner market on unique merchandise.

Major Competitors

Competitors in the Lynnville area are many—the River Road Strip has several gift shops and cafés. Each store strives to maintain individuality, but there is an abundance of crossover markets as well. Down by the River considers "Medusa's" and "Jigs and That" to be the two major competitors, strictly due to the size and volume of business. Down by the River has truly strived for an original inventory, unique to the River Road Strip.

Medusa's is a more upscale gift shop that features aromatherapy scented candles and incense. Asian-inspired clothing and décor items are the focus of their inventory. In addition, Medusa's offers silver and gold "trinket"-style jewelry in the price ranges of $20–$100. Prices are higher than average, and Medusa's typically draws tourist and environmentally conscious customers.

Jigs and That is a median-priced gift and sport shop that offers lower-end items, including river-inspired children's toys like fishing poles, nets, and sand toys. Also included in their inventory are more whimsical giftware and lower-end wares, similar to what is found in dollar stores and "five and dimes." Jigs and That also doubles as the local sporting goods store, where on the lower level you can find fishing poles, tackle, and fresh fishing bait. Life jackets, river rafts, and toys are also found here. Because of the largely male traffic, often accompanied by children, the sales are impulse, and most purchases are under $20.

To compete, Down by the River will, in turn, offer unique, often locally handcrafted jewelry that reflects river life. Prices will range from $5–$50, inspiring a more impulsive purchases in jewelry than offered at Medusa's. Focusing on local artisans, the giftware and art choices will be more unique than both Medusa's and Jigs and That. Offering upscale beachwear, sandals, and sunhats will compete with the lower-end T-shirts and caps found at Jigs and That. Wholly, Down by the River will strive to offer competitively priced merchandise that appeals to a wide array of customers. The slogan "Take a Little of the River Home" will truly be fulfilled — and at great prices.

MARKETING STRATEGY

Down by the River's marketing strategy will be to present itself as the newest gift shop in the Lynnville community and take advantage of the three-season tourist traffic brought by the Mississippi River.

Building and Signage

Given the highly visible position of the Granary Building on River Street, the sign will be a critical marketing tool. The exterior of the building will set the tone as a laid-back riverside store, with plenty of charm. The new sign will be large and highly visible to foot traffic as well as auto traffic on River Road.

Sales Strategy

We have established prices by taking into consideration the need to cover overhead, while maintaining competitiveness with the rest of the River Road proprietors. The goal is to become the most frequented, affordable gift shop on River Road by offering the most unique gifts at the most competitive prices. Our goal is to maintain 35 percent cost of goods sold and to maintain a net profit of over 15 percent before taxes.

Customer Service

Friendly, gracious service will be critical to ensuring repeat business. In a small community, word-of-mouth will be critical in maintaining a strong customer base and keeping an edge on the competition. Employees with a flair for decorating, salesmanship, and the "gift of gab" will make Down by the River a fun place to shop. Coffee, lemonade, and a sampling of treats (all for sale, of course!) will always be available.

Advertising and Promotions

In the month before our Grand Opening on May 10, 2007, we will target the local weekly newspapers and offer discount coupons. Local radio stations will promote the historic River Road shopping district and introduce its newest addition, Down by the River. These promotions will target local families and other permanent residents.

The second major component of our initial advertising and promotion efforts will be directed toward the estimated 10,000 tourists who visit Lynnville annually. We will advertise in tour guides that feature the Illinois river fronts as well as monthly "happenings" publications, to reach weekenders and other tourists.

Our advertising budget of $750 per month following the first four months of operation will be spent on print and radio advertising in the Lynnville area.

Media Objectives and Strategy

Our primary objective is to establish our image as a place to truly "Take a Little of the River Home" at affordable prices. We will maximize efficiency in the selection and scheduling of advertisements by:

- Selecting publications with the highest local market penetration, such as the *Lynnville Times* and the *River Road Shopper*.

- Collaborating with established businesses in the River Road shopping district to maximize advertising dollars.

- Purchasing more ad space during the holiday season and during special events like the annual art festival and the River Road shopping district's annual Christmas inserts.

The advertising campaigns will focus on unique offerings and historic location. We will support this plan with a consistent ad slogan: "Take a Little of the River Home."

Promotional Campaign

"Take a Little of the River Home" is the slogan that will hold our promotional campaign together. By tracking sales of promotional advertising and holding drawings for discounts and door prizes (enabling us to collect names and addresses for direct-mail marketing), we will be able to determine how we are reaching our target market.

E-Mail

The cheapest possible direct mail is e-mail. We will offer our patrons an opportunity to receive e-mail coupon offers on a monthly basis. E-mails will also include a thoughtful quote or saying.

Publicity Strategy

Down by the River will focus on the following publicity strategies:

- Developing an ongoing relationship with the editors of three local publications.

- Developing a regular and consistent promotional program targeting both local and transient populations.

- Completing a press kit to be used as the primary public relations tool for all target media contact.

Grand Opening

Down by the River will issue a series of press releases prior to the Grand Opening on May 10, 2007.

Publicity Revenues

We anticipate that at least 10 percent of our annual sales will be generated directly from our publicity. A full media kit will be sent to all local publications within the first two months of operation.

Community

Down by the River will sponsor a Youth Fishing Tournament in order to forge relationships with local families and residents. We will also participate in the annual Great River Road Art Festival to encourage relationships with locals and tourists alike.

OPERATING PROCEDURES

Location/Facility

Down by the River will be located at 1111 River Road in Lynnville, Illinois, a 1,200-square-foot building to be leased from the owner, Stephen Julius. Sophie Vanden has negotiated a lease agreement with Stephen Julius, with a rent of $575 a month for two years. The facility is zoned commercial and has previously housed a retail establishment, so little renovation is required.

The property is located on River Road, which is at the foot of Main Street and is the main thoroughfare for most traffic. It is within an hour of many larger communities, which makes Lynnville an ideal

When Sophie approached Becca with her idea about Down by the River, Becca could not refuse. Knowing the creativity and ambition Sophie had for her dream, Becca knew she needed to give the idea a try.

Responsibilities

Sophie Vanden and Becca Timpton will share responsibilities for management of day-to-day operations, purchasing, pricing, inventory control, and monitoring staff responsibilities.

In addition to managing everyday operations, Sophie's responsibilities will also include:

- Approval of all financial obligations.

- Planning, developing, and establishing customer-service policies and objectives.

- Establishing employee-relations policies.

- Managing marketing and advertising and plan promotions.

- Managing working capital and performing financial forecasting: budgeting, cash flow, pro-forma financial statements, and external financing.

- Preparing financial analysis of operations for guidance of management, including the preparation of reports which outline company's financial position in areas of income, expense, and earnings—all based on past, present, and future operations.

In addition to management of day-to-day operations, Becca will:

- Hire and train staff.

- Serve as liaison with artisans, consignors, and crafters.

Administrative Salaries

Sophie Vanden $32,000

Becca Timpton $28,000

FINANCIAL DATA

The financial data provided below is based on conservative estimates. The Grand Opening will be held in May of 2007.

To follow, we provide month-to-month operating budgets for the next five years.

The following are Down by the River's Five-Year Projected Revenue Goals.

FINANCIAL DOCUMENTS

Down by the River
Balance Sheet by Month—YEAR 1

	JAN	FEB	MAR	APRIL	MAY
ASSETS					
Cash	96,102	96,898	97,695	98,492	99,288
Inventory	8,000	8,000	8,000	8,000	8,000
Fixed Assets (Less Depreciation)	10,220	10,045	9,870	9,695	9,520
TOTAL	114,322	114,943	115,565	116,187	116,808
LIABILITIES & EQUITY					
CURRENT LIABILITIES:					
Accounts Payable	6,500	6,500	6,500	6,500	6,500
Credit Cards Payable	0	0	0	0	0
Payroll Taxes Payable	1,000	1,000	1,000	1,000	1,000
Sales Tax Payable	1,200	1,200	1,200	1,200	1,200
TOTAL CURRENT LIABILITIES	8,700	8,700	8,700	8,700	8,700
LONG-TERM LIABILITIES:					
NOTES PAYABLE	54,216	53,427	52,635	51,839	51,038
TOTAL LIABILITIES	62,916	62,127	61,335	60,539	59,738
EQUITY:					
Owner Investment	50,000	50,000	50,000	50,000	50,000
Retained Earnings	1,406	2,816	4,230	5,648	7,070
TOTAL EQUITY	51,406	52,816	54,230	55,648	57,070
TOTAL	114,322	114,943	115,565	116,187	116,808

JUNE	JULY	AUG	SEPT	OCT	NOV	DEC
100,084	100,880	101,677	102,474	103,271	104,067	87,722
8,000	8,000	8,000	8,000	8,000	8,000	8,000
9,345	9,170	8,995	8,820	8,645	8,470	8,295
117,429	118,050	118,672	119,294	119,916	120,537	104,017
6,500	6,500	6,500	6,500	6,500	6,500	6,500
0	0	0	0	0	0	0
1,000	1,000	1,000	1,000	1,000	1,000	1,000
1,200	1,200	1,200	1,200	1,200	1,200	1,200
8,700	8,700	8,700	8,700	8,700	8,700	8,700
50,233	49,424	48,611	47,794	46,973	46,147	45,317
58,933	58,124	57,311	56,494	55,673	54,847	54,017
50,000	50,000	50,000	50,000	50,000	50,000	50,000
8,496	9,926	11,361	12,800	14,243	15,690	0
58,496	59,926	61,361	62,800	64,243	65,690	50,000
117,429	118,050	118,672	119,294	119,916	120,537	104,017

243

Down by the River
Balance Sheet by Month—YEAR 3

	JAN	FEB	MAR	APRIL	MAY
ASSETS					
Cash	94,583	100,015	105,446	110,878	116,310
Inventory	8,000	8,000	8,000	8,000	8,000
Fixed Assets (Less Depreciation)	6,020	5,845	5,670	5,495	5,320
TOTAL	108,603	113,860	119,116	124,373	129,630
LIABILITIES & EQUITY					
CURRENT LIABILITIES:					
Accounts Payable	6,500	6,500	6,500	6,500	6,500
Credit Cards Payable	0	0	0	0	0
Payroll Taxes Payable	1,000	1,000	1,000	1,000	1,000
Sales Tax Payable	1,200	1,200	1,200	1,200	1,200
TOTAL CURRENT LIABILITIES	8,700	8,700	8,700	8,700	8,700
LONG-TERM LIABILITIES:					
NOTES PAYABLE	34,128	33,236	32,339	31,438	30,532
TOTAL LIABILITIES	42,828	41,936	41,039	40,138	39,232
EQUITY:					
Owner Investment	50,000	50,000	50,000	50,000	50,000
Retained Earnings	15,775	21,924	28,077	34,235	40,398
TOTAL EQUITY	65,775	71,924	78,077	84,235	90,398
TOTAL	108,603	113,860	119,116	124,373	129,630

JUNE	JULY	AUG	SEPT	OCT	NOV	DEC
121,741	127,173	132,605	138,036	143,467	148,899	79,731
8,000	8,000	8,000	8,000	8,000	8,000	8,000
5,145	4,970	4,795	4,620	4,445	4,270	4,095
134,886	140,143	145,400	150,656	155,912	161,169	91,826
6,500	6,500	6,500	6,500	6,500	6,500	6,500
0	0	0	0	0	0	0
1,000	1,000	1,000	1,000	1,000	1,000	1,000
1,200	1,200	1,200	1,200	1,200	1,200	1,200
8,700	8,700	8,700	8,700	8,700	8,700	8,700
29,621	28,706	27,786	26,861	25,931	24,997	24,058
38,321	37,406	36,486	35,561	34,631	33,697	32,758
50,000	50,000	50,000	50,000	50,000	50,000	50,000
46,565	52,737	58,914	65,095	71,281	77,472	9,068
96,565	102,737	108,914	115,095	121,281	127,472	59,068
134,886	140,143	145,400	150,656	155,912	161,169	91,826

Down by the River
Balance Sheet by Month—YEAR 5

	JAN	FEB	MAR	APRIL	MAY
ASSETS					
Cash	80,565	86,172	91,778	97,385	102,992
Inventory	8,000	8,000	8,000	8,000	8,000
Fixed Assets (Less Depreciation)	1,820	1,645	1,470	1,295	1,120
TOTAL	90,385	95,817	101,248	106,680	112,112
LIABILITIES & EQUITY					
CURRENT LIABILITIES:					
Accounts Payable	6,500	6,500	6,500	6,500	6,500
Credit Cards Payable	0	0	0	0	0
Payroll Taxes Payable	1,000	1,000	1,000	1,000	1,000
Sales Tax Payable	1,200	1,200	1,200	1,200	1,200
TOTAL CURRENT LIABILITIES	8,700	8,700	8,700	8,700	8,700
LONG-TERM LIABILITIES:					
NOTES PAYABLE	11,396	10,387	9,372	8,352	7,327
TOTAL LIABILITIES	20,096	19,087	18,072	17,052	16,027
EQUITY:					
Owner Investment	50,000	50,000	50,000	50,000	50,000
Retained Earnings	20,289	26,730	33,176	39,628	46,085
TOTAL EQUITY	70,289	76,730	83,176	89,628	96,085
TOTAL	90,385	95,817	101,248	106,680	112,112

JUNE	JULY	AUG	SEPT	OCT	NOV	DEC
108,598	114,204	119,811	125,417	131,024	136,631	40,238
8,000	8,000	8,000	8,000	8,000	8,000	8,000
945	770	595	420	245	70	0
117,543	122,974	128,406	133,837	139,269	144,701	48,238
6,500	6,500	6,500	6,500	6,500	6,500	6,500
0	0	0	0	0	0	0
1,000	1,000	1,000	1,000	1,000	1,000	1,000
1,200	1,200	1,200	1,200	1,200	1,200	1,200
8,700	8,700	8,700	8,700	8,700	8,700	8,700
6,296	5,260	4,219	3,172	2,120	1,063	0
14,996	13,960	12,919	11,872	10,820	9,763	8,700
50,000	50,000	50,000	50,000	50,000	50,000	25,000
52,547	59,014	65,487	71,965	78,449	84,938	14,538
102,547	109,014	115,487	121,965	128,449	134,938	39,538
117,543	122,974	128,406	133,837	139,269	144,701	48,238

Down by the River
Break-Even Analysis

Year One by Month							Aug-07	Sep-07	Oct-07
FIXED COSTS									
Operating Expenses									
Accounting/ Payroll Processing	500	500	500	500	500	500	500	500	500
Administrative Salaries	6,916	6,916	6,916	6,916	6,916	6,916	6,916	6,916	6,916
Administrative Office Expense	500	500	500	500	500	500	500	500	500
Advertising and Promotions	4,936	1,000	1,000	1,000	1,000	1,000	1,000	1,000	1,000
Bank Fees	100	100	100	100	100	100	100	100	100
Loan Interest Expense	675	666	657	648	639	630	620	611	601
Loan Principal Payment	1,193	1,202	1,211	1,220	1,229	1,239	1,248	1,257	1,267
Insurance	2,500	2,500	2,500	2,500	2,500	2,500	2,500	2,500	2,500
Exterminator	200	200	200	200	200	200	200	200	200
Lease Payment	2,000	2,000	2,000	2,000	2,000	2,000	2,000	2,000	2,000
Legal Fees	200	200	200	200	200	200	200	200	200
License and Permits	200	200	200	200	200	200	200	200	200
Payroll Staff	16,540	16,540	16,540	16,540	16,540	16,540	16,540	16,540	16,540
Real Estate Taxes	0	0	0	0	0	0	0	0	0
Repairs & Maintenance	1,000	1,000	1,000	1,000	1,000	1,000	1,000	1,000	1,000
Taxes Payroll FICA	1,794	1,794	1,794	1,794	1,794	1,794	1,794	1,794	1,794
Taxes Payroll FUTA	235	235	235	235	235	235	235	235	235
Taxes Payroll SUTA	469	469	469	469	469	469	469	469	469
Telephone	800	800	800	800	800	800	800	800	800

Nov-07	Dec-07	Jan-08	Feb-08	Mar-08	Apr-08	May-08	Jun-08	Jul-08	Year 1
500	500	500	500	500	500	500	500	500	6,000
6,916	6,916	6,916	6,916	6,916	6,916	6,916	6,916	6,916	82,992
500	500	500	500	500	500	500	500	500	6,000
1,000	1,000	1,000	1,000	1,000	1,000	1,000	1,000	1,000	15,936
100	100	100	100	100	100	100	100	100	1,200
592	582	573	620	611	601	592	582	573	7,494
1,276	1,286	1,295	1,248	1,257	1,267	1,276	1,286	1,295	14,925
2,500	2,500	2,500	2,500	2,500	2,500	2,500	2,500	2,500	30,000
200	200	200	200	200	200	200	200	200	2,400
2,000	2,000	2,000	2,000	2,000	2,000	2,000	2,000	2,000	24,000
200	200	200	200	200	200	200	200	200	2,400
200	200	200	200	200	200	200	200	200	2,400
16,540	16,540	16,540	16,540	16,540	16,540	16,540	16,540	16,540	198,482
0	0	0	0	0	0	0	0	0	0
1,000	1,000	1,000	1,000	1,000	1,000	1,000	1,000	1,000	12,000
1,794	1,794	1,794	1,794	1,794	1,794	1,794	1,794	1,794	21,533
235	235	235	235	235	235	235	235	235	2,815
469	469	469	469	469	469	469	469	469	5,629
800	800	800	800	800	800	800	800	800	9,600

Down by the River
Break-Even Analysis (continued)

YEAR ONE BY MONTH							Aug-07	Sep-07	Oct-07
FIXED COSTS (continued)									
Trash Removal	1,500	1,500	1,500	1,500	1,500	1,500	1,500	1,500	1,500
Utilities	2,000	2,000	2,000	2,000	2,000	2,000	2,000	2,000	2,000
Workers Comp.	1,525	1,525	1,525	1,525	1,525	1,525	1,525	1,525	1,525
Total Fixed Costs	45,783	41,847	41,847	41,847	41,847	41,847	41,847	41,847	41,847
VARIABLE COSTS									
Food COGS	13,110	13,110	13,110	13,110	13,110	13,110	13,110	13,110	13,110
Beverage COGS	4,471	4,471	4,471	4,471	4,471	4,471	4,471	4,471	4,471
Merchandise COGS	0	0	0	0	0	0	0	0	0
Credit Card Expense	1,042	1,042	1,042	1,042	1,042	1,042	1,042	1,042	1,042
Royalty Fees	0	0	0	0	0	0	0	0	0
Professional Fees/Other	200	200	200	200	200	200	200	200	200
Paper Supplies	1,500	1,500	1,500	1,500	1,500	1,500	1,500	1,500	1,500
Total Variable Costs	20,323	20,323	20,323	20,323	20,323	20,323	20,323	20,323	20,323
Income from Operations	71,880	71,880	71,880	71,880	71,880	71,880	71,880	71,880	71,880
INCOME FROM OPERATIONS ANALYSIS									
Contribution Margin	71.73%	71.73%	71.73%	71.73%	71.73%	71.73%	71.73%	71.73%	71.73%
Break-Even Sales Volume	63,831	58,343	58,343	58,343	58,343	58,343	58,343	58,343	58,343
Sales Volume Above Break-Even	8,049	13,537	13,537	13,537	13,537	13,537	13,537	13,537	13,537

Nov-07	Dec-07	Jan-08	Feb-08	Mar-08	Apr-08	May-08	Jun-08	Jul-08	Year 1
1,500	1,500	1,500	1,500	1,500	1,500	1,500	1,500	1,500	18,000
2,000	2,000	2,000	2,000	2,000	2,000	2,000	2,000	2,000	24,000
1,525	1,525	1,525	1,525	1,525	1,525	1,525	1,525	1,525	18,296
41,847	41,847	41,847	41,847	41,847	41,847	41,847	41,847	41,847	506,102
13,110	13,110	13,110	13,110	13,110	13,110	13,110	13,110	13,110	157,320
4,471	4,471	4,471	4,471	4,471	4,471	4,471	4,471	4,471	53,654
0	0	0	0	0	0	0	0	0	0
1,042	1,042	1,042	1,042	1,042	1,042	1,042	1,042	1,042	12,507
0	0	0	0	0	0	0	0	0	0
200	200	200	2 00	200	200	200	200	200	2,400
1,500	1,500	1,500	1,500	1,500	1,500	1,500	1,500	1,500	18,000
20,323	20,323	20,323	20,323	20,323	20,323	20,323	20,323	20,323	243,882
71,880	71,880	71,880	71,880	71,880	71,880	71,880	71,880	71,880	862,560
71.73%	71.73%	71.73%	71.73%	71.73%	71.73%	71.73%	71.73%	71.73%	71.73%
58,343	58,343	58,343	58,343	58,343	58,343	58,343	58,343	58,343	705,606
13,537	13,537	13,537	13,537	13,537	13,537	13,537	13,537	13,537	156,954

Down by the River
Projected Income Statement—YEAR 1

	JAN	FEB	MAR	APRIL	MAY
SALES	20,000	20,000	20,000	20,000	20,000
COST OF SALES	7,000	7,000	7,000	7,000	7,000
GROSS PROFIT	13,000	13,000	13,000	13,000	13,000
OPERATING EXPENSES					
Advertising	750	750	750	750	750
Bank & Credit Card Fees	50	50	50	50	50
Contract Labor	0	0	0	0	0
Dues & Subscriptions	25	25	25	25	25
Depreciation	175	175	175	175	175
Insurance	150	150	150	150	150
Interest	284	280	276	272	268
Office and Miscellaneous	200	200	200	200	200
Rent	575	575	575	575	575
Salaries - Officer	5,000	5,000	5,000	5,000	5,000
Salaries - Others	3,000	3,000	3,000	3,000	3,000
Supplies	100	100	100	100	100
Taxes & Licenses	800	800	800	800	800
Telephone	100	100	100	100	100
Other Expense	0	0	0	0	0
Other Expense	0	0	0	0	0
Other Expense	0	0	0	0	0
Other Expense	0	0	0	0	0
Other Expense	0	0	0	0	0
Other Expense	0	0	0	0	0
Total	11,209	11,205	11,201	11,197	11,193
OPERATING INCOME	1,791	1,795	1,799	1,803	1,807
OTHER INCOME:					
Misc Income	0	0	0	0	0
NET INCOME	1,791	1,795	1,799	1,803	1,807

JUNE	JULY	AUG	SEPT	OCT	NOV	DEC	TOTAL
20,000	20,000	20,000	20,000	20,000	20,000	30,000	250,000
7,000	7,000	7,000	7,000	7,000	7,000	10,500	87,500
13,000	13,000	13,000	13,000	13,000	13,000	19,500	162,500
750	750	750	750	750	750	750	9,000
50	50	50	50	50	50	50	600
0	0	0	0	0	0	0	0
25	25	25	25	25	25	25	300
175	175	175	175	175	175	175	2,100
150	150	150	150	150	150	150	1,800
264	260	255	251	247	243	238	3,138
200	200	200	200	200	200	200	2,400
575	575	575	575	575	575	575	6,900
5,000	5,000	5,000	5,000	5,000	5,000	5,000	60,000
3,000	3,000	3,000	3,000	3,000	3,000	3,000	36,000
100	100	100	100	100	100	100	1,200
800	800	800	800	800	800	800	9,600
100	100	100	100	100	100	100	1,200
0	0	0	0	0	0	0	0
0	0	0	0	0	0	0	0
0	0	0	0	0	0	0	0
0	0	0	0	0	0	0	0
0	0	0	0	0	0	0	0
0	0	0	0	0	0	0	0
11,189	11,185	11,180	11,176	11,172	11,168	11,163	134,238
1,811	1,815	1,820	1,824	1,828	1,832	8,337	28,262
0	0	0	0	0	0	0	0
1,811	1,815	1,820	1,824	1,828	1,832	8,337	28,262

Down by the River
Projected Income Statement—YEAR 2

	JAN	FEB	MAR	APRIL	MAY
SALES	25,000	25,000	25,000	25,000	25,000
COST OF SALES	8,750	8,750	8,750	8,750	8,750
GROSS PROFIT	16,250	16,250	16,250	16,250	16,250
OPERATING EXPENSES					
Advertising	750	750	750	750	750
Bank & Credit Card Fees	50	50	50	50	50
Contract Labor	0	0	0	0	0
Dues & Subscriptions	25	25	25	25	25
Depreciation	175	175	175	175	175
Insurance	150	150	150	150	150
Interest	234	230	225	221	217
Office and Miscellaneous	200	200	200	200	200
Rent	575	575	575	575	575
Salaries - Officer	5,000	5,000	5,000	5,000	5,000
Salaries - Others	3,000	3,000	3,000	3,000	3,000
Supplies	100	100	100	100	100
Taxes & Licenses	800	800	800	800	800
Telephone	100	100	100	100	100
Other Expense	0	0	0	0	0
Other Expense	0	0	0	0	0
Other Expense	0	0	0	0	0
Other Expense	0	0	0	0	0
Other Expense	0	0	0	0	0
Other Expense	0	0	0	0	0
Total	11,159	11,155	11,150	11,146	11,142
OPERATING INCOME	5,091	5,095	5,100	5,104	5,108
OTHER INCOME:					
Misc Income	0	0	0	0	0
NET INCOME	5,091	5,095	5,100	5,104	5,108

JUNE	JULY	AUG	SEPT	OCT	NOV	DEC	TOTAL
25,000	25,000	25,000	25,000	25,000	25,000	50,000	325,000
8,750	8,750	8,750	8,750	8,750	8,750	17,500	113,750
16,250	16,250	16,250	16,250	16,250	16,250	32,500	211,250
750	750	750	750	750	750	750	9,000
50	50	50	50	50	50	50	600
0	0	0	0	0	0	0	0
25	25	25	25	25	25	25	300
175	175	175	175	175	175	175	2,100
150	150	150	150	150	150	150	1,800
212	208	203	199	195	190	185	2,519
200	200	200	200	200	200	200	2,400
575	575	575	575	575	575	575	6,900
5,000	5,000	5,000	5,000	5,000	5,000	5,000	60,000
3,000	3,000	3,000	3,000	3,000	3,000	3,000	36,000
100	100	100	100	100	100	100	1,200
800	800	800	800	800	800	800	9,600
100	100	100	100	100	100	100	1,200
0	0	0	0	0	0	0	0
0	0	0	0	0	0	0	0
0	0	0	0	0	0	0	0
0	0	0	0	0	0	0	0
0	0	0	0	0	0	0	0
0	0	0	0	0	0	0	0
11,137	11,133	11,128	11,124	11,120	11,115	11,110	133,619
5,113	5,117	5,122	5,126	5,130	5,135	21,390	77,631
0	0	0	0	0	0	0	0
5,113	5,117	5,122	5,126	5,130	5,135	21,390	77,631

Down by the River
Projected Income Statement—YEAR 3

	JAN	FEB	MAR	APRIL	MAY
SALES	32,000	32,000	32,000	32,000	32,000
COST OF SALES	11,200	11,200	1,200	11,200	11,200
GROSS PROFIT	20,800	20,800	20,800	20,800	20,800
OPERATING EXPENSES					
Advertising	1,000	1,000	1,000	1,000	1,000
Bank & Credit Card Fees	50	50	50	50	50
Contract Labor	0	0	0	0	0
Dues & Subscriptions	25	25	25	25	25
Depreciation	175	175	175	175	175
Insurance	150	150	150	150	150
Interest	181	176	172	167	162
Office and Miscellaneous	200	200	200	200	200
Rent	575	575	575	575	575
Salaries - Officer	5,000	5,000	5,000	5,000	5,000
Salaries - Others	4,000	4,000	4,000	4,000	4,000
Supplies	200	200	200	200	200
Taxes & Licenses	900	900	900	900	900
Telephone	100	100	100	100	100
Other Expense	0	0	0	0	0
Other Expense	0	0	0	0	0
Other Expense	0	0	0	0	0
Other Expense	0	0	0	0	0
Other Expense	0	0	0	0	0
Other Expense	0	0	0	0	0
Total	12,556	12,551	12,547	12,542	12,537
OPERATING INCOME	8,244	8,249	8,253	8,258	8,263
OTHER INCOME:					
Misc Income	0	0	0	0	0
NET INCOME	8,244	8,249	8,253	8,258	8,263

JUNE	JULY	AUG	SEPT	OCT	NOV	DEC	TOTAL
32,000	32,000	32,000	32,000	32,000	32,000	48,000	400,000
11,200	11,200	11,200	11,200	11,200	11,200	16,800	140,000
20,800	20,800	20,800	20,800	20,800	20,800	31,200	260,000
1,000	1,000	1,000	1,000	1,000	1,000	1,000	12,000
50	50	50	50	50	50	50	600
0	0	0	0	0	0	0	0
25	25	25	25	25	25	25	300
175	175	175	175	175	175	175	2,100
150	150	150	150	150	150	150	1,800
158	153	148	144	139	134	129	1,863
200	200	200	200	200	200	200	2,400
575	575	575	575	575	575	575	6,900
5,000	5,000	5,000	5,000	5,000	5,000	5,000	60,000
4,000	4,000	4,000	4,000	4,000	4,000	4,000	48,000
200	200	200	200	200	200	200	2,400
900	900	900	900	900	900	900	10,800
100	100	100	100	100	100	100	1,200
0	0	0	0	0	0	0	0
0	0	0	0	0	0	0	0
0	0	0	0	0	0	0	0
0	0	0	0	0	0	0	0
0	0	0	0	0	0	0	0
0	0	0	0	0	0	0	0
12,533	12,528	12,523	12,519	12,514	12,509	12,504	150,363
8,267	8,272	8,277	8,281	8,286	8,291	18,696	109,637
0	0	0	0	0	0	0	0
8,267	8,272	8,277	8,281	8,286	8,291	18,696	109,637

Down by the River
Projected Income Statement—YEAR 4

	JAN	FEB	MAR	APRIL	MAY
SALES	38,000	38,000	38,000	38,000	38,000
COST OF SALES	13,300	13,300	13,300	13,300	13,300
GROSS PROFIT	24,700	24,700	24,700	24,700	24,700
OPERATING EXPENSES					
Advertising	1,250	1,250	1,250	1,250	1,250
Bank & Credit Card Fees	50	50	50	50	50
Contract Labor	0	0	0	0	0
Dues & Subscriptions	50	50	50	50	50
Depreciation	175	175	175	175	175
Insurance	250	250	250	250	250
Interest	124	119	115	110	105
Office and Miscellaneous	500	500	500	500	500
Rent	575	575	575	575	575
Salaries - Officer	6,000	6,000	6,000	6,000	6,000
Salaries - Others	5,000	5,000	5,000	5,000	5,000
Supplies	400	400	400	400	400
Taxes & Licenses	1,200	1,200	1,200	1,200	1,200
Telephone	200	200	200	200	200
Other Expense	0	0	0	0	0
Other Expense	0	0	0	0	0
Other Expense	0	0	0	0	0
Other Expense	0	0	0	0	0
Other Expense	0	0	0	0	0
Other Expense	0	0	0	0	0
Total	15,774	15,769	15,765	15,760	15,755
OPERATING INCOME	8,926	8,931	8,935	8,940	8,945
OTHER INCOME:					
Misc Income	0	0	0	0	0
NET INCOME	8,926	8,931	8,935	8,940	8,945

JUNE	JULY	AUG	SEPT	OCT	NOV	DEC	TOTAL
38,000	38,000	38,000	38,000	38,000	38,000	57,000	475,000
13,300	13,300	13,300	13,300	13,300	13,300	19,950	166,250
24,700	24,700	24,700	24,700	24,700	24,700	37,050	308,750
1,250	1,250	1,250	1,250	1,250	1,250	1,250	15,000
50	50	50	50	50	50	50	600
0	0	0	0	0	0	0	0
50	50	50	50	50	50	50	600
175	175	175	175	175	175	175	2,100
250	250	250	250	250	250	250	3,000
100	95	90	85	79	74	69	1,165
500	500	500	500	500	500	500	6,000
575	575	575	575	575	575	575	6,900
6,000	6,000	6,000	6,000	6,000	6,000	6,000	72,000
5,000	5,000	5,000	5,000	5,000	5,000	5,000	60,000
400	400	400	400	400	400	400	4,800
1,200	1,200	1,200	1,200	1,200	1,200	1,200	14,400
200	200	200	200	200	200	200	2,400
0	0	0	0	0	0	0	0
0	0	0	0	0	0	0	0
0	0	0	0	0	0	0	0
0	0	0	0	0	0	0	0
0	0	0	0	0	0	0	0
0	0	0	0	0	0	0	0
15,750	15,745	15,740	15,735	15,729	15,724	15,719	184,965
8,950	8,955	8,960	8,965	8,971	8,976	21,331	119,785
0	0	0	0	0	0	0	0
8,950	8,955	8,960	8,965	8,971	8,976	21,331	119,785

Down by the River
Projected Income Statement—YEAR 5

	JAN	FEB	MAR	APRIL	MAY
SALES	40,000	40,000	40,000	40,000	40,000
COST OF SALES	14,000	14,000	14,000	14,000	14,000
GROSS PROFIT	26,000	26,000	26,000	26,000	26,000
OPERATING EXPENSES					
Advertising	1,500	1,500	1,500	1,500	1,500
Bank & Credit Card Fees	50	50	50	50	50
Contract Labor	0	0	0	0	0
Dues & Subscriptions	50	50	50	50	50
Depreciation	175	175	175	175	175
Insurance	500	500	500	500	500
Interest	64	59	54	48	43
Office and Miscellaneous	650	650	650	650	650
Rent	575	575	575	575	575
Salaries - Officer	6,500	6,500	6,500	6,500	6,500
Salaries - Others	5,000	5,000	5,000	5,000	5,000
Supplies	600	600	600	600	600
Taxes & Licenses	1,200	1,200	1,200	1,200	1,200
Telephone	200	200	200	200	200
Other Expense	0	0	0	0	0
Other Expense	0	0	0	0	0
Other Expense	0	0	0	0	0
Other Expense	0	0	0	0	0
Other Expense	0	0	0	0	0
Other Expense	0	0	0	0	0
Total	17,064	17,059	17,054	17,048	17,043
OPERATING INCOME	8,936	8,941	8,946	8,952	8,957
OTHER INCOME:					
Misc Income	0	0	0	0	0
NET INCOME	8,936	8,941	8,946	8,952	8,957

JUNE	JULY	AUG	SEPT	OCT	NOV	DEC	TOTAL
40,000	40,000	40,000	40,000	40,000	40,000	60,000	500,000
14,000	14,000	14,000	14,000	14,000	14,000	21,000	175,000
26,000	26,000	26,000	26,000	26,000	26,000	39,000	325,000
1,500	1,500	1,500	1,500	1,500	1,500	1,500	18,000
50	50	50	50	50	50	50	600
0	0	0	0	0	0	0	0
50	50	50	50	50	50	50	600
175	175	175	175	175	175	70	1,995
500	500	500	500	500	500	500	6,000
38	33	27	22	16	11	5	420
650	650	650	650	650	650	650	7,800
575	575	575	575	575	575	575	6,900
6,500	6,500	6,500	6,500	6,500	6,500	6,500	78,000
5,000	5,000	5,000	5,000	5,000	5,000	5,000	60,000
600	600	600	600	600	600	600	7,200
1,200	1,200	1,200	1,200	1,200	1,200	1,200	14,400
200	200	200	200	200	200	200	2,400
0	0	0	0	0	0	0	0
0	0	0	0	0	0	0	0
0	0	0	0	0	0	0	0
0	0	0	0	0	0	0	0
0	0	0	0	0	0	0	0
0	0	0	0	0	0	0	0
17,038	17,033	17,027	17,022	17,016	17,011	16,900	204,315
8,962	8,967	8,973	8,978	8,984	8,989	22,100	120,712
0	0	0	0	0	0	0	0
8,962	8,967	8,973	8,978	8,984	8,989	22,100	120,712

Down by the River
Projected Statements of Cash Flow—YEAR 1

NET INCOME	1,791	1,795	1,799	1,803	1,807
NON-CASH EXPENSES:					
Depreciation	175	175	175	175	175
FIXED ASSET PURCHASES:	(10,395)	0	0	0	0
INVENTORY:					
Beginning	0	8,000	8,000	8,000	8,000
Ending	(8,000)	(8,000)	(8,000)	(8,000)	(8,000)
ACCOUNTS PAYABLE:					
Beginning	0	(6,500)	(6,500)	(6,500)	(6,500)
Ending	6,500	6,500	6,500	6,500	6,500
CREDIT CARDS PAYABLE:					
Beginning	0	0	0	0	0
Ending	0	0	0	0	0
PAYROLL TAXES PAYABLE:					
Beginning	0	(1,000)	(1,000)	(1,000)	(1,000)
Ending	1,000	1,000	1,000	1,000	1,000
SALES TAX PAYABLE:					
Beginning	0	(1,200)	(1,200)	(1,200)	(1,200)
Ending	1,200	1,200	1,200	1,200	1,200
NOTE PAYABLE:					
Beginning	0	(54,216)	(53,427)	(52,635)	(51,839)
Ending	54,216	53,427	52,635	51,839	51,038
OWNER INVESTMENT:					
Beginning	0	(50,000)	(50,000)	(50,000)	(50,000)
Ending	50,000	50,000	50,000	50,000	50,000
DIVIDENDS	0	0	0	0	0
INCOME TAXES	(385)	(385)	(385)	(385)	(385)
CHANGE IN CASH	96,102	796	797	797	796
CASH - BEGINNING	0	96,102	96,898	97,695	98,492
CASH - ENDING	96,102	96,898	97,695	98,492	99,288
Cash Check - Digit	0.00	0.00	0.00	0.00	0.00

Cash on balance sheet must match ending cash on cash flow statement.

1,811	1,815	1,820	1,824	1,828	1,832	8,337
175	175	175	175	175	175	175
0	0	0	0	0	0	0
8,000	8,000	8,000	8,000	8,000	8,000	8,000
(8,000)	(8,000)	(8,000)	(8,000)	(8,000)	(8,000)	(8,000)
(6,500)	(6,500)	(6,500)	(6,500)	(6,500)	(6,500)	(6,500)
6,500	6,500	6,500	6,500	6,500	6,500	6,500
0	0	0	0	0	0	0
0	0	0	0	0	0	0
(1,000)	(1,000)	(1,000)	(1,000)	(1,000)	(1,000)	(1,000)
1,000	1,000	1,000	1,000	1,000	1,000	1,000
(1,200)	(1,200)	(1,200)	(1,200)	(1,200)	(1,200)	(1,200)
1,200	1,200	1,200	1,200	1,200	1,200	1,200
(51,038)	(50,233)	(49,424)	(48,611)	(47,794)	(46,973)	(46,147)
50,233	49,424	48,611	47,794	46,973	46,147	45,317
(50,000)	(50,000)	(50,000)	(50,000)	(50,000)	(50,000)	(50,000)
50,000	50,000	50,000	50,000	50,000	50,000	50,000
0	0	0	0	0	0	(23,642)
(385)	(385)	(385)	(385)	(385)	(385)	(385)
796	796	797	797	797	796	(16,345)
99,288	100,084	100,880	101,677	102,474	103,271	104,067
100,084	100,880	101,677	102,474	103,271	104,067	87,722
0.00	0.00	0.00	0.00	0.00	0.00	0.00

Down by the River
Projected Statements of Cash Flow—YEAR 2

NET INCOME	5,091	5,095	5,100	5,104	5,108
NON-CASH EXPENSES:					
Depreciation	175	175	175	175	175
FIXED ASSET PURCHASES:	0	0	0	0	0
INVENTORY:					
Beginning	8,000	8,000	8,000	8,000	8,000
Ending	(8,000)	(8,000)	(8,000)	(8,000)	(8,000)
ACCOUNTS PAYABLE:					
Beginning	(6,500)	(6,500)	(6,500)	(6,500)	(6,500)
Ending	6,500	6,500	6,500	6,500	6,500
CREDIT CARDS PAYABLE:					
Beginning	0	0	0	0	0
Ending	0	0	0	0	0
PAYROLL TAXES PAYABLE:					
Beginning	(1,000)	(1,000)	(1,000)	(1,000)	(1,000)
Ending	1,000	1,000	1,000	1,000	1,000
SALES TAX PAYABLE:					
Beginning	(1,200)	(1,200)	(1,200)	(1,200)	(1,200)
Ending	1,200	1,200	1,200	1,200	1,200
NOTE PAYABLE:					
Beginning	(45,317)	(44,482)	(43,644)	(42,801)	(41,954)
Ending	44,482	43,644	42,801	41,954	41,102
OWNER INVESTMENT:					
Beginning	(50,000)	(50,000)	(50,000)	(50,000)	(50,000)
Ending	50,000	50,000	50,000	50,000	50,000
DIVIDENDS	0	0	0	0	0
INCOME TAXES	(1,500)	(1,500)	(1,500)	(1,500)	(1,500)
CHANGE IN CASH	2,931	2,932	2,932	2,932	2,931
CASH - BEGINNING	87,722	90,653	93,585	96,517	99,449
CASH - ENDING	90,653	93,585	96,517	99,449	102,380
Cash Check - Digit	0.00	0.00	0.00	0.00	0.00

Cash on balance sheet must match ending cash on cash flow statement.

5,113	5,117	5,122	5,126	5,130	5,135	21,390
175	175	175	175	175	175	175
0	0	0	0	0	0	0
8,000	8,000	8,000	8,000	8,000	8,000	8,000
(8,000)	(8,000)	(8,000)	(8,000)	(8,000)	(8,000)	(8,000)
(6,500)	(6,500)	(6,500)	(6,500)	(6,500)	(6,500)	(6,500)
6,500	6,500	6,500	6,500	6,500	6,500	6,500
0	0	0	0	0	0	0
0	0	0	0	0	0	0
(1,000)	(1,000)	(1,000)	(1,000)	(1,000)	(1,000)	(1,000)
1,000	1,000	1,000	1,000	1,000	1,000	1,000
(1,200)	(1,200)	(1,200)	(1,200)	(1,200)	(1,200)	(1,200)
1,200	1,200	1,200	1,200	1,200	1,200	1,200
(41,102)	(40,246)	(39,385)	(38,520)	(37,651)	(36,777)	(35,899)
40,246	39,385	38,520	37,651	36,777	35,899	35,016
(50,000)	(50,000)	(50,000)	(50,000)	(50,000)	(50,000)	(50,000)
50,000	50,000	50,000	50,000	50,000	50,000	50,000
0	0	0	0	0	0	(50,000)
(1,500)	(1,500)	(1,500)	(1,500)	(1,500)	(1,500)	(1,500)
2,932	2,931	2,932	2,932	2,931	2,932	(30,818)
102,380	105,312	108,243	111,175	114,107	117,038	119,970
105,312	108,243	111,175	114,107	117,038	119,970	89,152
0.00	0.00	0.00	0.00	0.00	0.00	0.00

Down by the River
Projected Statements of Cash Flow—YEAR 3

NET INCOME	8,244	8,249	8,253	8,258	8,263
NON-CASH EXPENSES:					
Depreciation	175	175	175	175	175
FIXED ASSET PURCHASES:	0	0	0	0	0
INVENTORY:					
Beginning	8,000	8,000	8,000	8,000	8,000
Ending	(8,000)	(8,000)	(8,000)	(8,000)	(8,000)
ACCOUNTS PAYABLE:					
Beginning	(6,500)	(6,500)	(6,500)	(6,500)	(6,500)
Ending	6,500	6,500	6,500	6,500	6,500
CREDIT CARDS PAYABLE:					
Beginning	0	0	0	0	0
Ending	0	0	0	0	0
PAYROLL TAXES PAYABLE:					
Beginning	(1,000)	(1,000)	(1,000)	(1,000)	(1,000)
Ending	1,000	1,000	1,000	1,000	1,000
SALES TAX PAYABLE:					
Beginning	(1,200)	(1,200)	(1,200)	(1,200)	(1,200)
Ending	1,200	1,200	1,200	1,200	1,200
NOTE PAYABLE:					
Beginning	(35,016)	(34,128)	(33,236)	(32,339)	(31,438)
Ending	34,128	33,236	32,339	31,438	30,532
OWNER INVESTMENT:					
Beginning	(50,000)	(50,000)	(50,000)	(50,000)	(50,000)
Ending	50,000	50,000	50,000	50,000	50,000
DIVIDENDS	0	0	0	0	0
INCOME TAXES	(1,200)	(1,200)	(1,200)	(1,200)	(1,200)
CHANGE IN CASH	5,431	5,432	5,431	5,432	5,432
CASH - BEGINNING	89,152	94,583	100,015	105,446	110,878
CASH - ENDING	94,583	100,015	105,446	110,878	116,310
Cash Check - Digit	0.00	0.00	0.00	0.00	0.00

Cash on balance sheet must match ending cash on cash flow statement.

8,267	8,272	8,277	8,281	8,286	8,291	18,696
175	175	175	175	175	175	175
0	0	0	0	0	0	0
8,000	8,000	8,000	8,000	8,000	8,000	8,000
(8,000)	(8,000)	(8,000)	(8,000)	(8,000)	(8,000)	(8,000)
(6,500)	(6,500)	(6,500)	(6,500)	(6,500)	(6,500)	(6,500)
6,500	6,500	6,500	6,500	6,500	6,500	6,500
0	0	0	0	0	0	0
0	0	0	0	0	0	0
(1,000)	(1,000)	(1,000)	(1,000)	(1,000)	(1,000)	(1,000)
1,000	1,000	1,000	1,000	1,000	1,000	1,000
(1,200)	(1,200)	(1,200)	(1,200)	(1,200)	(1,200)	(1,200)
1,200	1,200	1,200	1,200	1,200	1,200	1,200
(30,532)	(29,621)	(28,706)	(27,786)	(26,861)	(25,931)	(24,997)
29,621	28,706	27,786	26,861	25,931	24,997	24,058
(50,000)	(50,000)	(50,000)	(50,000)	(50,000)	(50,000)	(50,000)
50,000	50,000	50,000	50,000	50,000	50,000	50,000
0	0	0	0	0	0	(85,000)
(2,100)	(2,100)	(2,100)	(2,100)	(2,100)	(2,100)	(2,100)
5,431	5,432	5,432	5,431	5,431	5,432	(69,168)
116,310	121,741	127,173	132,605	138,036	143,467	148,899
121,741	127,173	132,605	138,036	143,467	148,899	79,731
0.00	0.00	0.00	0.00	0.00	0.00	0.00

Down by the River
Projected Statements of Cash Flow—YEAR 4

NET INCOME	8,926	8,931	8,935	8,940	8,945
NON-CASH EXPENSES:					
Depreciation	175	175	175	175	175
FIXED ASSET PURCHASES:	0	0	0	0	0
INVENTORY:					
Beginning	8,000	8,000	8,000	8,000	8,000
Ending	(8,000)	(8,000)	(8,000)	(8,000)	(8,000)
ACCOUNTS PAYABLE:					
Beginning	(6,500)	(6,500)	(6,500)	(6,500)	(6,500)
Ending	6,500	6,500	6,500	6,500	6,500
CREDIT CARDS PAYABLE:					
Beginning	0	0	0	0	0
Ending	0	0	0	0	0
PAYROLL TAXES PAYABLE:					
Beginning	(1,000)	(1,000)	(1,000)	(1,000)	(1,000)
Ending	1,000	1,000	1,000	1,000	1,000
SALES TAX PAYABLE:					
Beginning	(1,200)	(1,200)	(1,200)	(1,200)	(1,200)
Ending	1,200	1,200	1,200	1,200	1,200
NOTE PAYABLE:					
Beginning	(24,058)	(23,114)	(22,165)	(21,211)	(20,252)
Ending	23,114	22,165	21,211	20,252	19,288
OWNER INVESTMENT:					
Beginning	(50,000)	(50,000)	(50,000)	(50,000)	(50,000)
Ending	50,000	50,000	50,000	50,000	50,000
DIVIDENDS	0	0	0	0	0
INCOME TAXES	(2,500)	(2,500)	(2,500)	(2,500)	(2,500)
CHANGE IN CASH	5,657	5,657	5,656	5,656	5,656
CASH - BEGINNING	79,731	85,388	91,045	96,701	102,357
CASH - ENDING	85,388	91,045	96,701	102,357	108,013
Cash Check - Digit	0.00	0.00	0.00	0.00	0.00

Cash on balance sheet must match ending cash on cash flow statement.

5,113	5,117	5,122	5,126	5,130	5,135	21,390
175	175	175	175	175	175	175
0	0	0	0	0	0	0
8,000	8,000	8,000	8,000	8,000	8,000	8,000
(8,000)	(8,000)	(8,000)	(8,000)	(8,000)	(8,000)	(8,000)
(6,500)	(6,500)	(6,500)	(6,500)	(6,500)	(6,500)	(6,500)
6,500	6,500	6,500	6,500	6,500	6,500	6,500
0	0	0	0	0	0	0
0	0	0	0	0	0	0
(1,000)	(1,000)	(1,000)	(1,000)	(1,000)	(1,000)	(1,000)
1,000	1,000	1,000	1,000	1,000	1,000	1,000
(1,200)	(1,200)	(1,200)	(1,200)	(1,200)	(1,200)	(1,200)
1,200	1,200	1,200	1,200	1,200	1,200	1,200
(41,102)	(40,246)	(39,385)	(38,520)	(37,651)	(36,777)	(35,899)
40,246	39,385	38,520	37,651	36,777	35,899	35,016
(50,000)	(50,000)	(50,000)	(50,000)	(50,000)	(50,000)	(50,000)
50,000	50,000	50,000	50,000	50,000	50,000	50,000
0	0	0	0	0	0	(50,000)
(1,500)	(1,500)	(1,500)	(1,500)	(1,500)	(1,500)	(1,500)
2,932	2,931	2,932	2,932	2,931	2,932	(30,818)
102,380	105,312	108,243	111,175	114,107	117,038	119,970
105,312	108,243	111,175	114,107	117,038	119,970	89,152
0.00	0.00	0.00	0.00	0.00	0.00	0.00

Down by the River
Projected Statements of Cash Flow – YEAR 5

NET INCOME	8,936	8,941	8,946	8,952	8,957
NON-CASH EXPENSES:					
Depreciation	175	175	175	175	175
FIXED ASSET PURCHASES:	0	0	0	0	0
INVENTORY:					
Beginning	8,000	8,000	8,000	8,000	8,000
Ending	(8,000)	(8,000)	(8,000)	(8,000)	(8,000)
ACCOUNTS PAYABLE:					
Beginning	(6,500)	(6,500)	(6,500)	(6,500)	(6,500)
Ending	6,500	6,500	6,500	6,500	6,500
CREDIT CARDS PAYABLE:					
Beginning	0	0	0	0	0
Ending	0	0	0	0	0
PAYROLL TAXES PAYABLE:					
Beginning	(1,000)	(1,000)	(1,000)	(1,000)	(1,000)
Ending	1,000	1,000	1,000	1,000	1,000
SALES TAX PAYABLE:					
Beginning	(1,200)	(1,200)	(1,200)	(1,200)	(1,200)
Ending	1,200	1,200	1,200	1,200	1,200
NOTE PAYABLE:					
Beginning	(12,401)	(11,396)	(10,387)	(9,372)	(8,352)
Ending	11,396	10,387	9,372	8,352	7,327
OWNER INVESTMENT:					
Beginning	(50,000)	(50,000)	(50,000)	(50,000)	(50,000)
Ending	50,000	50,000	50,000	50,000	50,000
DIVIDENDS	0	0	0	0	0
INCOME TAXES	(2,500)	(2,500)	(2,500)	(2,500)	(2,500)
CHANGE IN CASH	30,606	5,607	5,606	5,607	5,607
CASH - BEGINNING	49,959	80,565	86,172	91,778	97,385
CASH - ENDING	80,565	86,172	91,778	97,385	102,992
Cash Check - Digit	0.00	0.00	0.00	0.00	0.00

Cash on balance sheet must match ending cash on cash flow statement.

8,962	8,967	8,973	8,978	8,984	8,989	22,100
175	175	175	175	175	175	175
0	0	0	0	0	0	0
8,000	8,000	8,000	8,000	8,000	8,000	8,000
(8,000)	(8,000)	(8,000)	(8,000)	(8,000)	(8,000)	(8,000)
(6,500)	(6,500)	(6,500)	(6,500)	(6,500)	(6,500)	(6,500)
6,500	6,500	6,500	6,500	6,500	6,500	6,500
0	0	0	0	0	0	0
0	0	0	0	0	0	0
(1,000)	(1,000)	(1,000)	(1,000)	(1,000)	(1,000)	(1,000)
1,000	1,000	1,000	1,000	1,000	1,000	1,000
(1,200)	(1,200)	(1,200)	(1,200)	(1,200)	(1,200)	(1,200)
1,200	1,200	1,200	1,200	1,200	1,200	1,200
(7,327)	(6,296)	(5,260)	(4,219)	(3,172)	(2,120)	(1,063)
6,296	5,260	4,219	3,172	2,120	1,063	0
(50,000)	(50,000)	(50,000)	(50,000)	(50,000)	(50,000)	(50,000)
50,000	50,000	50,000	50,000	50,000	50,000	50,000
0	0	0	0	0	0	(50,000)
(2,500)	(2,500)	(2,500)	(2,500)	(2,500)	(2,500)	(2,500)
5,606	5,606	5,607	5,606	5,607	5,607	(96,393)
102,992	108,598	114,204	119,811	125,417	131,024	136,631
108,598	114,204	119,811	125,417	131,024	136,631	40,238
0.00	0.00	0.00	0.00	0.00	0.00	0.00

Down by the River
Operating Budget Summary Years 1–5

For the Year Ending	JUL-07	JUL-08	JUL-08	JUL-10	JUL-11
SALES					
Food	629,280	786,600	943,920	1,089,540	1,089,540
Beverage	233,280	108,000	129,600	137,700	137,700
Merchandise	0	0	0	0	0
Total Sales	862,560	894,600	1,073,520	1,227,240	1,227,240
		4%	20%	14%	0%
COST OF SALES					
Food	157,320	196,650	235,980	272,385	272,385
Beverage	53,654	24,840	29,808	31,671	31,671
Merchandise	0	0	0	0	0
Total Cost Of Sales	210,974	221,490	265,788	304,056	304,056
% of Total Sales	24.46%	24.76%	24.76%	24.78%	24.78%
Gross Profit	651,586	673,110	807,732	923,184	923,184
% of Total Sales	75.54%	75.24%	75.24%	75.22%	75.22%
OPERATING EXPENSES					
Accounting/Payroll Processing	6,000	6,300	6,615	6,946	7,293
Administrative Salaries	82,992	82,992	82,992	82,992	82,992
Administrative Office Expenses	6,000	6,300	6,615	6,946	7,293
Advertising & Promotions	59,232	62,194	65,303	68,568	71,997
Bank Fees	1,200	1,260	1,323	1,389	1,459
Credit Card Expense	12,507	12,972	15,566	17,795	17,795
Loan Interest Expense	7,494	6,094	4,563	2,888	1,056
Principal Loan Payment	14,925	16,325	17,856	2,888	21,204
Insurance/Fire/Theft/ Liability/Liquor/ Product	30,000	31,500	33,075	34,729	36,465
Exterminator	2,400	2,520	2,646	2,778	2,917
Legal Fees	2,400	2,520	2,646	2,778	2,917

For the Year Ending	JUL-07	JUL-08	JUL-08	JUL-10	JUL-11
OPERATING EXPENSES (continued)					
Licenses and Permits	2,400	2,520	2,646	2,778	2,917
Royalty Fees	0	0	0	0	0
Payroll/Staff	198,482	208,406	218,826	229,768	241,256
Professional Fees/Other	2,400	2,520	2,646	2,778	2,917
Paper Supplies	18,000	18,900	19,845	20,837	21,879
Lease Payment	24,000	25,200	26,460	27,783	29,172
Repairs and Maintenance	12,000	12,600	13,230	13,892	14,586
Trash Removal	18,000	18,900	19,845	20,837	21,879
Real Estate Taxes (CEMC)	0	0	0	0	0
Taxes Payroll/FICA	21,533	22,292	23,089	23,926	24,805
Taxes Payroll/FUTA	2,815	2,914	3,018	3,128	3,242
Taxes Payroll/SUTA	5,629	5,828	6,036	6,255	6,485
Telephone	9,600	10,080	10,584	11,113	11,669
Utilities	24,000	25,200	26,460	27,783	29,172
Workers' Compensation	18,296	18,941	19,618	20,329	21,076
Total Operating Expenses	582,305	605,277	631,505	641,905	684,445
% of Total Sales	67.51%	67.66%	58.83%	52.30%	55.77%
Total Expenses	793,279	826,767	897,293	945,961	988,501
% of Total Sales	91.97%	92.42%	83.58%	77.08%	80.55%
Net Profit Before Income Taxes	69,281	67,833	176,227	281,279	238,739
% of Total Sales	8.03%	7.58%	16.42%	22.92%	19.45%
Taxes on Income	19,399	18,993	63,442	109,699	85,946
% of Total Sales	2.25%	2.12%	5.91%	8.94%	7.00%
Net Income After Taxes	49,882	48,840	112,785	171,580	152,793
% of Total Sales	5.78%	5.46%	10.51%	13.98%	12.45%

Down by the River
Income Statements Summary Years 1–5

	JUL-07	JUL-08	JUL-08	JUL-10	JUL-11
SALES					
Food	629,280	786,600	943,920	1,089,540	1,089,540
Beverage	233,280	108,000	129,600	137,700	137,700
Merchandise	0	0	0	0	0
Total Sales	862,560	894,600	1,073,520	1,227,240	1,227,240
COST OF SALES					
Food	157,320	196,650	235,980	272,385	272,385
Beverage	53,654	24,840	29,808	31,671	31,671
Merchandise	0	0	0	0	0
Total Cost of Goods Sold	210,974	221,490	265,788	304,056	304,056
% of Total Sales	24.46%	24.76%	24.76%	24.78%	24.78%
Gross Profit	651,586	673,110	807,732	923,184	923,184
% of Total Sales	75.54%	75.24%	75.24%	75.22%	75.22%
OPERATING EXPENSES					
Operating Expenses (without Depreciation)	567,380	588,952	613,648	639,017	663,240
Depreciation	31,428	31,428	31,428	31,428	31,428
Total Operating Expenses	598,808	620,380	645,076	670,445	694,668
% of Total Sales	69.42%	69.35%	60.09%	54.63%	56.60%
Total Expenses	809,783	841,870	910,864	974,501	998,724
% of Total Sales	93.88%	94.11%	84.85%	79.41%	81.38%
Income From Operations	52,777	52,730	162,656	252,739	228,516
% of Total Sales	6.12%	5.89%	15.15%	20.59%	18.62%
Taxes on Income	14,778	14,764	58,556	90,986	82,266
% of Total Sales	1.71%	1.65%	5.45%	7.41%	6.70%
Net Income After Taxes	37,999	37,966	104,100	161,753	146,250
% of Total Sales	4.41%	4.24%	9.70%	13.18%	11.92%
EBITDA	91,700	90,252	198,647	287,055	260,999
% of Total Sales	10.63%	10.09%	18.50%	23.39%	21.27%

Down by the River
Balance Sheets Summary Years 1–5

For the Month Ending	JUL-07	JUL-08	JUL-08	JUL-10	JUL-11
ASSETS					
Current Assets					
Cash	615,124	689,344	860,015	1,074,413	1,198,830
Investments	0	0	0	0	0
Inventory	1,734	1,820	2,185	2,499	2,499
Other Current Assets	8,525	8,525	8,525	8,525	8,525
Total Current Assets	625,383	699,689	870,725	1,085,437	1,209,854
Fixed Assets					
Land	0	0	0	0	0
Buildings	0	0	0	0	0
Building/Leasehold Improvements	16,750	16,750	16,750	16,750	16,750
Restaurant Equipment	155,000	155,000	155,000	155,000	155,000
Furniture	48,250	48,250	48,250	48,250	48,250
Delivery Van/ Automobiles	0	0	0	0	0
Goodwill	0	0	0	0	0
Less Accumulated Depreciation	(31,428)	(62,856)	(94,284)	(125,712)	(157,140)
Total Fixed Assets	188,572	157,144	125,716	94,288	62,860
Other Assets	0	0	0	0	0
Total Assets	813,955	856,833	996,441	1,179,725	1,272,714
LIABILITIES					
Current Liabilities					
Short-Term Debt	24,568	24,568	24,568	24,568	0
Accounts Payable	66,107	87,355	96,923	105,555	82,374
Notes Payable/ Mortgage	0	0	0	0	0
Other Payables	5,000	5,000	5,000	5,000	5,000
Accrued Liabilities	0	0	0	0	0
Total Current Liabilities	95,675	116,923	126,491	135,123	87,374

For the Month Ending	JUL-07	JUL-08	JUL-08	JUL-10	JUL-11
LIABILITIES (continued)					
Long Term Debt	75,075	58,751	40,894	21,363	0
Total Liabilities	170,750	175,674	167,385	156,486	87,374
Owner/Stockholder Equity					
Owners' Equity Common Stock	250,000	250,000	250,000	250,000	250,000
Retained Earnings	34,797	72,765	179,358	331,702	479,240
Earnings Distributed/ Dividends Paid	0	0	0	0	0
Total Owners' Equity	288,001	325,969	433,471	595,224	741,474
Total Liabilities and Equity	813,955	856,833	996,441	1,179,725	1,272,714

GLOSSARY

A

ACCOUNTANT A person skilled in maintaining and auditing financial records.

ACCOUNTING PERIOD A period of time, such as a quarter or year, for which a financial statement is produced.

ACCOUNTS PAYABLE Amounts owed to providers and creditors by a business.

ACCOUNTS RECEIVABLE An accounting entry that represents an entity's obligation to pay cash to its creditors.

ADVERTISING Purchase of space, time, or printed matter for the purpose of increasing sales.

AGREEMENT A contract between two or more people guaranteeing each party something from the other party.

AMBIANCE Sounds, sights, smells, and attitude of an operation.

ASSET Everything owned by a company that has profitable or redeemable value.

B

BALANCE SHEET A financial statement that reports a company's assets and liabilities at a specific point in time.

BREAK-EVEN POINT The point at which no profit is made because the sales equal the costs.

BUSINESS ENTITY An organization that possesses a separate existence for tax purposes.

BUSINESS PLAN A summary that explains the vision, objectives, needs, and necessary steps to become a successful business.

BUSINESS PROFILE A business description and definition.

C

CAPITAL Any cash, funds, assets, and accounts that the business currently possesses.

CLOSELY HELD CORPORATION A nonpublic corporation that is owned by a small number of shareholders.

COMMISSION A fee paid based on the amount of sales personally derived.

COMPENSATION Something given in return for a service or a value.

CONSIGNMENT PRODUCTS Items provided to a company by a vendor who charges for them after they are used.

D

DEFAULT A breach of contract; failure to pay on a promissory note when due.

DISCLOSURE DOCUMENT The statement that must be provided to prospective customers that describes trading strategy, fees, performance, etc.

E

EBITDA Earnings Before Interest, Taxes, Depreciation and Amortization; A measure of income to debt ratio.

ENTREPRENEUR A person who organizes, operates, and assumes the risk for a business venture.

EXPENDITURE Amount spent on goods and services.

F

FAIR MARKET VALUE The price of a commodity or service at which both buyers and sellers agree to do business.

FINANCIAL STATEMENTS A record of a business's financial flows and levels that typically include a balance sheet, an income statement or a profit and loss statement, a cash flow statement, and a statement of retained earnings.

FRANCHISE An arrangement for the rights of a particular trademark, trade name, product, and copyright to be used in a certain location for a certain amount of time.

FRANCHISOR The owner of

the franchise that grants the franchisees rights to sell its products and use its name.

G

GENERAL PARTNERSHIP A partnership in which each of the partners is liable for all of the business's debt.

I

INCOME STATEMENT A statement showing the profit or loss of a business.

INCORPORATION Creating a new corporation.

INDUSTRY The specific branch of manufacture and trade.

INVENTORY CONTROLS Methods and policies designed to prevent fraud, minimize errors, promote operating efficiency, and achieve compliance with established policies.

L

LIABILITY Debt or obligation owed by the company.

LIMITED LIABILITY COMPANY A business structure created so that the owners are only liable to the extent of their contribution.

LIQUIDATION The sale of assets to pay off debts.

LOCATION The site where

the business will operate.

LOGO A name, symbol, or trademark designed for easy and definite recognition.

M

MANUAL Guidebook for employees and managers outlining the company policies.

MARGIN The difference between the cost and the selling price of securities or commodities.

MARKETING Means by which an outlet is exposed to the public.

MARKETING PLAN A business plan, marketing strategy, and anticipated expansion of the business.

MONETARY To do with currency or coinage.

N

NET CASH FLOW The revenue remaining after costs, interest, and debts are paid.

NET WORTH The difference between total assets and liabilities.

O

OFFER A proposal to buy a business.

OFFICERS A person having administrative or managerial authority in an organization.

OPERATING BUDGET A budget that applies to all outlays other than capital outlays.

OUTSOURCING The procuring of services or products from an outside supplier or manufacturer in order to cut costs.

OVERHEAD The operating expenses of a business, including the costs of rent, utilities, and taxes.

OWNER The person who possesses complete control over the business.

P

PARTNERSHIP A business entity in which two or more agree to furnish a part of the capital and labor for a business enterprise, and by which each shares a fixed proportion of profits and losses.

PRO FORMA A hypothetical balance sheet and income statement based on a set of assumptions; used in earnings reports.

PROCEDURE The method of doing a task.

PROFIT & LOSS STATEMENT A statement showing the income and expenses of the business.

R

REAL PROPERTY All

immovable property such as land and buildings or other objects permanently affixed to the land.

RECEIPT A written acknowledgement that something has been received.

RENEWAL A re-signing of a franchise agreement when the past contract expires.

RISK The possibility that actual outcomes may differ from those expected.

ROYALTY A share in the proceeds paid to an inventor or a proprietor for the right to use his or her invention or services.

S

S.C.O.R.E. Service Corps of Retired Executives; a nonprofit organization that provides small business counseling.

SALARY A regular payment for services rendered.

SBA Small Business Administration; agency that provides support to small businesses.

SECTOR A group of securities that share common characteristics.

SHARE One of a finite number of equal portions in the capital of a company, entitling the owner to a proportion of distributed profits and to a portion of the value of the company in case of liquidation.

SHAREHOLDER One that owns or holds a share or shares of stock; a stockholder.

SOLE PROPRIETORSHIP A business organization that is unincorporated and has only one owner.

STOCK The number of shares that each stockholder possesses.

STOCK CERTIFICATE A document stating proof of ownership of stock in a corporation.

SWEAT EQUITY Non-cash value added to real estate by the owner, such as do-it-yourself improvements.

T

TRADEMARK An officially registered name, symbol, or other device identifying a product that is protected against others' use.

V

VARIABLE COST The fluctuating cost of doing business that is directly related to the sales of goods or services.

W

WORKING CAPITAL The excess of current assets over current liabilities of any business at any time.

INDEX

DID YOU BORROW THIS COPY?

Have you been borrowing a copy of *How to Write a Great Business Plan for Your Small Business in 60 Minutes or Less* from a friend, colleague, or library? Wouldn't you like your own copy for quick and easy reference? To order, photocopy the form below and send to:

Atlantic Publishing Company
1210 SW 23rd Place
Ocala, FL 34474-7014